Sweater Weather

by Tammy Kreimeyer

10 Cute and Comfy Designs to Keep You Warm

LEISURE ARTS, INC. • Maumelle, Arkansas

Contents

EASY

Hooded Pullover

Shopping List

Yarn (Bulky Weight) BULKY 5
[6 ounces, 185 yards
(170 grams, 169 meters) per skein]:

1a. Short Sleeve Version
- ☐ {4-4}{5-5-5} skeins

1b. Long Sleeve Version
- ☐ {4-5}{5-5-6} skeins

Knitting Needles
Straight,
- ☐ Size 10½ (6.5 mm) **or** size needed for gauge

29" (73.5 cm) Circular,
- ☐ Size 10½ (6.5 mm)

Additional Supplies
- ☐ Markers - 3
- ☐ Yarn needle
- ☐ Sewing needle & matching thread
- ☐ ⅞" (22 mm) Buttons - 3

Size Information

Finished Chest Measurement:
{34-36}{38½-41-43½}"/
{86.5-91.5}{98-104-110.5} cm

Size Note: We have printed the instructions for the sizes in different colors to make it easier for you to find:

- size Small in Blue
- size Medium in Pink
- size Large in Green
- size 1X in Purple
- size 2X in Red

Instructions in Black apply to all sizes.

Gauge Information

In Stockinette Stitch
(knit one row, purl one row),
13 sts and 17 rows = 4" (10 cm)

Techniques Used

- Increasing Evenly Spaced ***(page 45)***
- Knit increase ***(Figs. 2a & b, page 46)***
- K2 tog ***(Fig. 6, page 46)***
- Slip 1, K1, PSSO ***(Figs. 8a & b, pages 46 & 47)***

Back

Band

Cast on {57-61}{65-69-73} sts.

Rows 1-10: K1, (P1, K1) across.

Body

Beginning with a **knit** row, work in Stockinette Stitch until Back measures approximately {19-19½}{20-20½-21}"/{48.5-49.5}{51-52-53.5} cm from cast on edge, ending by working a **purl** row.

Shoulder Shaping

Rows 1-4: Bind off {6-7}{8-9-10} sts at the beginning of the row, work across: 33 sts.

Bind off remaining sts.

Front

Work same as Back until Front measures approximately 10½" (26.5 cm) from cast on edge, ending by working a **purl** row.

Placket Opening

Row 1: Knit {26-28}{30-32-34} sts, bind off next 5 sts; knit across: {26-28}{30-32-34} sts **each** side.

Note: Both sides of Placket Opening are worked at the same time, using separate yarn for **each** side.

Work even until Front measures same as Back to Shoulder Shaping, ending by working a **purl** row.

Shoulder Shaping

Rows 1-4: Bind off {6-7}{8-9-10} sts at Armhole edge, work across; with second yarn, work across, do **not** cut yarn: 14 sts **each** side.

Hood

Row 1: Slip 14 sts from left Front onto circular needle; cut yarn on left Front only; with same circular needle, knit across right Front, holding Back with **right** side facing, pick up 33 sts across Back neck edge ***(Figs. 12a & b, page 47)***, knit across left Front: 61 sts.

Rows 2-10: Beginning with a **purl** row, work in Stockinette Stitch for 9 rows.

Row 11: K 29, knit increase, K1, knit increase, knit across: 63 sts.

Rows 12-20: Beginning with a **purl** row, work in Stockinette Stitch for 9 rows.

Row 21: K 30, knit increase, K1, knit increase, knit across: 65 sts.

Rows 22-30: Beginning with a **purl** row, work in Stockinette Stitch for 9 rows.

Row 31: K 31, knit increase, K1, knit increase, knit across: 67 sts.

Rows 32-40: Beginning with a **purl** row, work in Stockinette Stitch for 9 rows.

Row 41: K 32, knit increase, K1, knit increase, knit across: 69 sts.

Work even until Hood measures approximately 11" (28 cm), ending by working a **purl** row.

Shaping

Row 1: K 29, bind off next 11 sts, knit across: 29 sts **each** side.

Note: Both sides are worked at the same time, using separate yarn for **each** side.

Rows 2-5: Work across; with second yarn, bind off 5 sts, work across: 19 sts **each** side.

Bind off remaining sts.

Short Sleeve Version A (Make 2)

Band

Cast on {39-39}{41-43-43} sts.

Rows 1-8: K1, (P1, K1) across.

Row 9 (Right side): Knit across increasing 6 sts evenly spaced: {45-45}{47-49-49} sts.

Body

Beginning with a **purl** row, work in Stockinette Stitch increasing one stitch at each edge, every fourth row, {2-1}{3-2-7} time(s); then increase every sixth row, {3-4}{3-4-1} time(s): {55-55}{59-61-65} sts.

Work even until Sleeve measures approximately {10-10½}{11-11½-12}"/{25.5-26.5}{28-29-30.5} cm from cast on edge, ending by working a **purl** row.

Bind off all sts in **knit**.

Long Sleeve Version B (Make 2)

Band

Cast on {21-21}{23-25-25} sts.

Rows 1-8: K1, (P1, K1) across.

Row 9 (Right side)**:** Knit across increasing {8-8}{8-8-10} sts evenly spaced: {29-29}{31-33-35} sts.

Body

Beginning with a **purl** row, work in Stockinette Stitch increasing one stitch at each edge, every fourth row, {13-13}{14-14-15} times: {55-55}{59-61-65} sts.

Work even until Sleeve measures approximately {17-17½}{17½-18-18½}"/{43-44.5}{44.5-45.5-47} cm from cast on edge, ending by working a **purl** row.

Bind off all sts in **knit**.

Finishing

Sew top Hood seam.
Sew shoulder seams.

Button Placket

With **right** side facing, using circular needle and beginning at right Front Placket Opening, pick up {131-133}{137-139-143} sts evenly spaced around to bound off sts.

Rows 1-3: K1, (P1, K1) across.

Place 3 markers on right front Button Placket for buttonhole placement, placing first marker in stitch corresponding with shoulder seam, second marker 1" (2.5 cm) from bound off stitches, and third marker evenly spaced between first and second markers.

Row 4 (Buttonhole Row)**:** (Work across to next marker, bind off next st in pattern) 3 times, work across.

Row 5: ★ Work across to bound off st; turn, add on one st ***(Figs. 5a & b, page 46)***; **turn**; repeat from ★ 2 times **more**, work across.

Rows 6 and 7: K1, (P1, K1) across.

Bind off remaining sts in pattern.

Sew Button Placket to bound off stitches on Front. Sew buttons opposite buttonholes.

Pouch

Cast on {43-47}{51-55-59} sts.

Row 1: K1, (P1, K1) twice, purl across to last 5 sts, K1, (P1, K1) twice.

Row 2 (Right side)**:** (K1, P1) twice, knit across to last 4 sts, (P1, K1) twice.

Rows 3-11: Repeat Rows 1 and 2, 4 times; then repeat Row 1 once **more**.

Row 12 (Decrease row)**:** (K1, P1) twice, slip 1 as if to **knit**, K1, PSSO, knit across to last 6 sts, K2 tog, (P1, K1) twice: {41-45}{49-53-57} sts.

Rows 13-15: Repeat Rows 1 and 2 once, then repeat Row 1 once **more**.

Repeat Rows 12-15 until Pouch measures approximately 6½" (16.5 cm) from cast on edge, ending by working a **right** side row.

Last 7 Rows: K1, (P1, K1) across.

Bind off remaining sts in pattern.

Sew Pouch to Front, sewing cast on edge of Pouch just above Band and sew bound off edge to Front ½" (12 mm) below Button Placket.

Sew Sleeves to Sweater, matching center of last row on Sleeve to shoulder seam and beginning {8½-8½}{9-9½-10}"/{21.5-21.5}{23-24-25.5} cm down from seam.

Weave underarm and side in one continuous seam *(Fig. 13, page 47)*.

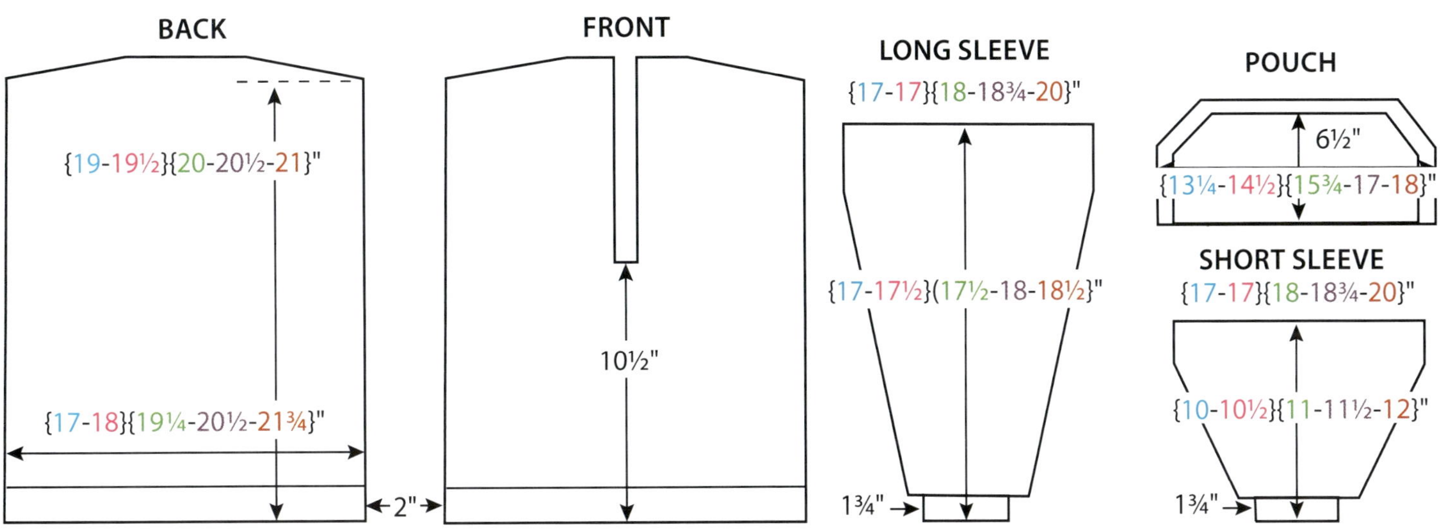

EASY

Hooded Zippered Cardigan

Shopping List

Yarn (Bulky Weight) BULKY 5
[6 ounces, 185 yards
(170 grams, 169 meters) per skein]:
- ☐ {4-4}{5-5-6} skeins

Knitting Needles
Straight,
- ☐ Size 10½ (6.5 mm) **or** size needed for gauge

Additional Supplies
- ☐ Stitch holder - 2
- ☐ Yarn needle
- ☐ Sewing needle & matching thread
- ☐ {18-18}{20-20-20}"/ {45.5-45.5}{51-51-51}
- ☐ Separating zipper

Size Information

Finished Chest Measurement:
{34½-37}{39½-42-44}"/
{87.5-94}{100.5-106.5-112} cm

Size Note: We have printed the instructions for the sizes in different colors to make it easier for you to find:

- size Small in Blue
- size Medium in Pink
- size Large in Green
- size 1X in Purple
- size 2X in Red

Instructions in Black apply to all sizes.

Gauge Information

With larger size needles,
in Reverse Stockinette Stitch
(purl one row, knit one row),
13 sts and 17 rows = 4" (10 cm)

Techniques Used

- Increasing Evenly Spaced ***(page 45)***
- Knit increase ***(Figs. 2a & b, page 46)***
- K2 tog ***(Fig. 6, page 46)***

Stitch Guide

TWIST (uses next 2 sts)
K2 tog leaving stitches on left needle, then knit the first stitch, slipping both stitches off the needle.

Back

Ribbing

With larger size needles, cast on {58-62}{66-70-74} sts.

Row 1: K2, (P2, K2) across.

Row 2 (Right side)**:** P2, (K2, P2) across.

Row 3: K2, (P2, K2) across.

Row 4: P2, (work Twist, P2) across.

Rows 5-12: Repeat Rows 1-4 twice.

Body

Beginning with a **knit** row, work in Reverse Stockinette Stitch until Back measures approximately {17-17}{19-19-19}"/{43-43}{48.5-48.5-48.5} cm from cast on edge, ending by working a **knit** row.

Shoulder Shaping

Rows 1 and 2: Bind off {7-7}{8-9-10} sts at the beginning of the row, work across: {44-48}{50-52-54} sts.

Rows 3 and 4: Bind off {7-8}{8-9-10} sts at the beginning of the row, work across: {30-32}{34-34-34} sts.

Slip remaining sts onto st holder.

Left Front

Ribbing

With larger size needles, cast on {29-29}{33-33-37} sts.

Row 1: K1, (P2, K2) across.

Row 2 (Right side)**:** (P2, K2) across to last st, P1.

Row 3: K1, (P2, K2) across.

Row 4: (P2, work Twist) across to last st, P1.

Rows 5-12: Repeat Rows 1-4 twice.

Body

Row 1: Knit across increasing {0-2}{0-2-0} sts evenly spaced *(see Zeros, page 45)*: {29-31}{33-35-37} sts.

Beginning with a **purl** row, work in Reverse Stockinette Stitch until Left Front measures same as Back to Shoulder Shaping, ending by working a **knit** row.

Shoulder Shaping

Row 1: Bind off {7-7}{8-9-10} sts, purl across: {22-24}{25-26-27} sts.

Row 2: Knit across.

Row 3: Bind off {7-8}{8-9-10} sts, purl across: {15-16}{17-17-17} sts.

Slip remaining sts onto st holder.

Right Front

Ribbing

With larger size needles, cast on {29-29}{33-33-37} sts.

Row 1: (K2, P2) across to last st, K1.

Row 2 (Right side)**:** P1, (K2, P2) across.

Row 3: (K2, P2) across to last st, K1.

Row 4: P1, (work Twist, P2) across.

Rows 5-12: Repeat Rows 1-4 twice.

Body

Row 1: Knit across increasing {0-2}{0-2-0} sts evenly spaced: {29-31}{33-35-37} sts.

Beginning with a **purl** row, work in Reverse Stockinette Stitch until Right Front measures same as Back to Shoulder Shaping, ending by working a **purl** row.

Shoulder Shaping

Row 1: Bind off {7-7}{8-9-10} sts, knit across: {22-24}{25-26-27} sts.

Row 2: Purl across.

Row 3: Bind off {7-8}{8-9-10} sts, knit across; do **not** cut yarn: {15-16}{17-17-17} sts.

Hood

Row 1 (Right side): Add on 3 sts (for Casing) ***(Figs. 5a & b, page 46)***, purl across, holding Back with **right** side facing, slip {30-32}{34-34-34} sts from st holder onto empty needle and purl across, purl across {15-16}{17-17-17} sts from Left Front st holder; **turn**, add on 3 sts (for Casing): {66-70}{74-74-74} sts.

Rows 2-9: Beginning with a **knit** row, work in Reverse Stockinette Stitch for 8 rows.

Row 10: Knit {31-33}{35-35-35} sts, knit increase, K2, knit increase, knit across: {68-72}{76-76-76} sts.

Rows 11-19: Beginning with a **purl** row, work in Reverse Stockinette Stitch for 9 rows.

Row 20: Knit {32-34}{36-36-36} sts, knit increase, K2, knit increase, knit across: {70-74}{78-78-78} sts.

Rows 21-29: Beginning with a **purl** row, work in Reverse Stockinette Stitch for 9 rows.

Row 30: Knit {33-35}{37-37-37} sts, knit increase, K2, knit increase, knit across: {72-76}{80-80-80} sts.

Rows 31-39: Beginning with a **purl** row, work in Reverse Stockinette Stitch for 9 rows.

Row 40: Knit {34-36}{38-38-38} sts, knit increase, K2, knit increase, knit across: {74-78}{82-82-82} sts.

Work even until Hood measures approximately 11" (28 cm), ending by working a **knit** row.

Shaping

Row 1: Purl {32-34}{36-36-36} sts, bind off next 10 sts, purl across: {32-34}{36-36-36} sts **each** side.

Note: Both sides are worked at same time, using separate yarn for **each** side.

Rows 2-5: Work across; with second yarn, bind off 5 sts, work across: {22-24}{26-26-26} sts **each** side.

Bind off remaining sts.

Sleeve (Make 2)

Ribbing

With larger size needles, cast on {26-26}{30-30-30} sts.

Row 1: K2, (P2, K2) across.

Row 2 (Right side): P2, (K2, P2) across.

Row 3: K2, (P2, K2) across.

Row 4: P2, (work Twist, P2) across.

Rows 5-8: Repeat Rows 1-4.

Body

Row 1: Knit across increasing 6 sts evenly spaced: {32-32}{36-36-36} sts.

Beginning with a **purl** row, work in Reverse Stockinette Stitch increasing one stitch at **each** edge, every fourth row, {7-9}{8-14-16} times; then increase every sixth row, {5-4}{5-1-0} time(s): {56-58}{62-66-68} sts.

Work even until Sleeve measures approximately {17-17½}{18-18-18½}"/{43-44.5}{45.5-45.5-47} cm from cast on edge.

Bind off all sts.

Finishing

Sew top Hood seam.
Sew shoulder seams.

Sew Sleeves to Cardigan, matching center of last row on Sleeve to shoulder seam and beginning {8½-9}{9½-10-10½}"/{21.5-23}{24-25.5-26.5} cm down from seam.

Weave underarm and side in one continuous seam *(Fig. 13, page 47)*.

Sew in zipper.

Fold Casing to **wrong** side of Hood and sew in place leaving bottom edges unsewn.

Twisted Cord

Cut 2 pieces of yarn, each **3 times** longer than the desired finished length. Holding both pieces together, fasten one end to a stationary object **or** have another person hold it; twist until **tight**. Fold in half and let it twist itself, knot both ends and cut the loops on the folded end.

Thread Twisted Cord through Casing on Hood.

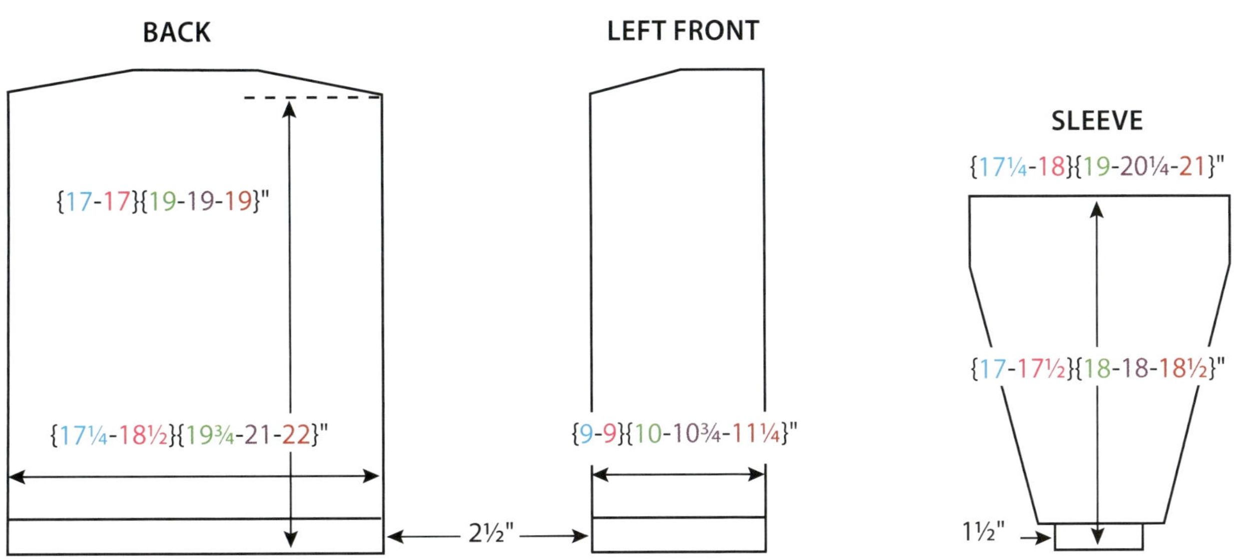

EASY

Funnel Neck Pullover

Shopping List

Yarn (Bulky Weight) BULKY 5
[6 ounces, 185 yards
(170 grams, 169 meters) per skein]:
☐ {4-5}{5-5-6} skeins

Knitting Needles
Straight,
☐ Size 10½ (6.5 mm) **or** size needed for gauge
16" (40.5 cm) Circular,
☐ Size 9 (5.5 mm)

Additional Supplies
☐ Stitch holders - 2
☐ Marker
☐ Yarn needle

Size Information

Finished Chest Measurement:
{37-39}{41-43-45}"/
{94-99}{104-109-114.5} cm

Size Note: We have printed the instructions for the sizes in different colors to make it easier for you to find:

- size Small in Blue
- size Medium in Pink
- size Large in Green
- size 1X in Purple
- size 2X in Red

Instructions in Black apply to all sizes.

Gauge Information

With larger size needles, in Stockinette Stitch (knit one row, purl one row), 13 sts and 17 rows = 4" (10 cm)

Techniques Used

- Increases ***(pages 45 & 46)***
- YO ***(Fig. 4, page 46)***
- K2 tog ***(Fig. 6, page 46)***
- Slip 1, K1, PSSO ***(Figs. 8a & b, pages 46 & 47)***

Back

Band

With larger size needles, cast on {62-66}{69-72-75} sts.

Rows 1-10: Knit across.

Body

Beginning with a **purl** row, work in Stockinette Stitch until Back measures approximately {13-13½}{14-14½-15}"/{33-34.5}{35.5-37-38} cm from cast on edge, ending by working a **purl** row.

Armhole Shaping

Rows 1 and 2: Bind off {3-3}{4-4-4} sts at the beginning of the row, work across: {56-60}{61-64-67} sts.

Row 3 (Decrease row)**:** K1, slip 1 as if to **knit**, K1, PSSO, knit across to last 3 sts, K2 tog, K1: {54-58}{59-62-65} sts.

Row 4: Purl across.

Rows 5 thru {6-6}{6-8-8}: Repeat Rows 3 and 4, {2-2}{2-3-3} times: {50-54}(55-56-59} sts.

Work even until Armholes measure approximately {9½-9½}{10-10-10½}"/{24-24}{25.5-25.5-26.5} cm, ending by working a **knit** row.

Shoulder Shaping

Rows 1 and 2: Bind off {6-7}{7-7-8} sts at the beginning of the row, work across: {38-40}{41-42-43} sts.

Rows 3 and 4: Bind off {6-7}(8-8-9} sts at the beginning of the row, work across: {26-26}{25-26-25} sts.

Slip remaining sts onto st holder.

Front

Work same as Back until Armholes measure approximately {6¼-6¼}{6½-6¾-7}"/{16-16}{16.5-17-18} cm, ending by working a **knit** row.

Neck Shaping

Note: Both sides of Neck are worked at the same time, using separate yarn for **each** side.

Row 1: Purl {17-19}{20-20-22} sts, slip next {16-16}{15-16-15} sts onto st holder; with second yarn, purl across: {17-19}{20-20-22} sts **each** side.

Row 2 (Decrease row)**:** Knit across to within 2 sts of Neck edge, K2 tog; with second yarn, slip 1 as if to **knit**, K1, PSSO, knit across: {16-18}{19-19-21} sts **each** side.

Row 3: Purl across; with second yarn, purl across.

Rows 4-11: Repeat Rows 2 and 3, 4 times: {12-14}{15-15-17} sts **each** side.

Work even until Armholes measure same as Back to Shoulder Shaping, ending by working a **knit** row.

Shoulder Shaping

Rows 1 and 2: Bind off {6-7}{7-7-8} sts at Armhole edge, work across; with second yam, work across: {6-7}{8-8-9} sts **each** side.

Row 3: Bind off remaining sts on first side; with second yarn, purl across.

Bind off remaining sts.

Sleeve (Make 2)

Band

With larger size needles, cast on {26-28}{30-32-34} sts.

Rows 1-7: Knit across.

Row 8: Knit across increasing 8 sts evenly spaced: {34-36}{38-40-42} sts.

Body

Beginning with a **purl** row, work in Stockinette Stitch increasing one stitch at each edge, every twelfth row, 5 times: {44-46}{48-50-52} sts.

Work even until Sleeve measures approximately {17½-17½} {17½-18-18½}"/(44.5-44.5} {44.5-45.5-47} cm from cast on edge, ending by working a **purl** row.

Sleeve Cap

Rows 1 and 2: Bind off {3-3}{4-4-4} sts at the beginning of the row, work across: {38-40}{40-42-44} sts.

Row 3 (Decrease row)**:** K1, slip 1 as if to **knit**, K1, PSSO, knit across to last 3 sts, K2 tog, K1: {36-38}{38-40-42} sts.

Row 4: Purl across.

Rows 5 thru {6-6}{6-8-8}: Repeat Rows 3 and 4, {2-2}{2-3-3} times: {32-34}{34-34-36} sts.

Work even until Sleeve Cap measures approximately {6-6}{6-6½-6½}"/ {15-15}{15-16.5-16.5} cm, ending by working a **purl** row.

Next 6 Rows: Bind off 4 sts at the beginning of the row, work across: {8-10}{10-10-12} sts.

Bind off remaining sts.

Finishing

Sew shoulder seams.

Neck Edging

With **right** side facing and using circular needle, knit {26-26}{25-26-25} sts from Back st holder, pick up {14-14}{16-18-20} sts evenly spaced along left Front Neck edge ***(Fig. 12a, page 47)***, knit {16-16}{15-16-15} sts from Front st holder, pick up {14-14}{16-18-20} sts evenly spaced along right Front Neck edge, place marker to indicate the beginning of rnd ***(see Markers, page 45)***: {70-70}{72-78-80} sts.

Rnd 1: Purl around.

Rnd 2: Knit around.

Rnd 3: Purl around.

Rnds 4 and 5: Knit around.

Rnd 6: (K2 tog, YO) around.

Rnds 7 and 8: Knit around.

Rnds 9-11: Repeat Rnds 1-3.

Bind off all sts **loosely** in **knit**.

Set in Sleeves, matching center of Sleeve Cap to shoulder seam.

Weave underarm and side in one continuous seam ***(Fig. 13, page 47)***.

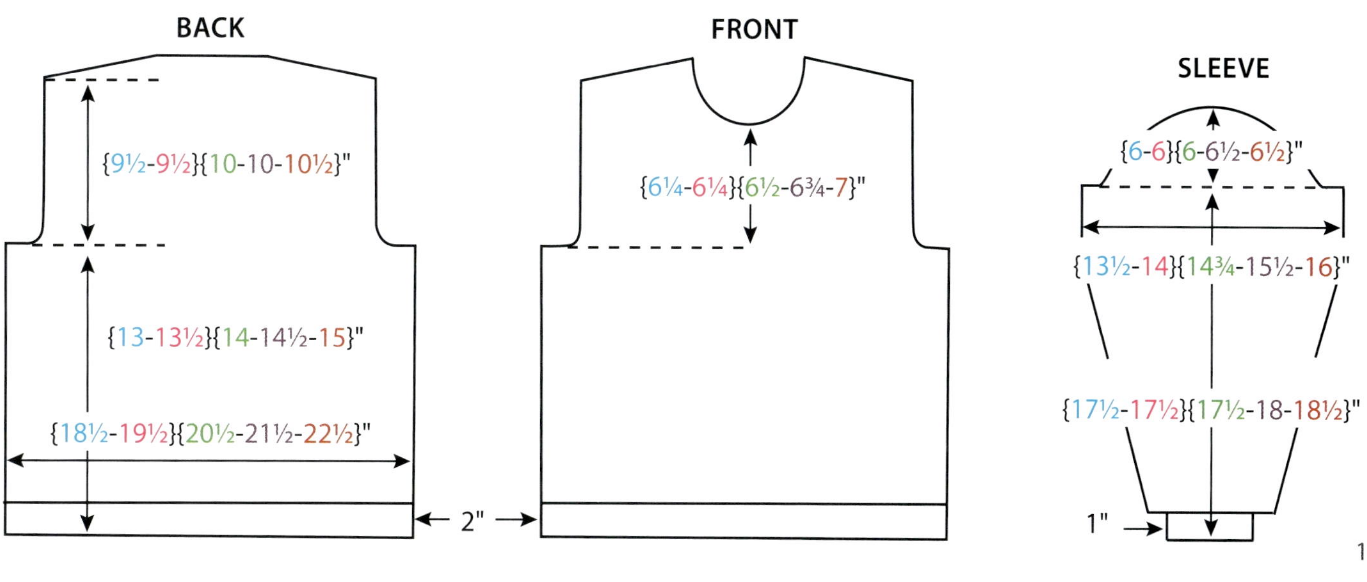

EASY

Cardigan Vest

Shopping List

Yarn (Bulky Weight) BULKY 5
[6 ounces, 185 yards
(170 grams, 169 meters) per skein]:
- ☐ MC (Tan) - 2{3-3} skeins
- ☐ CC (Blue) - 1{2-2} skein(s)

Knitting Needles
Straight,
- ☐ Size 10 (6 mm) **or** size needed for gauge

29" (73.5 cm) Circular,
- ☐ Size 8 (5 mm)

Additional Supplies
- ☐ Marker
- ☐ Yarn needle
- ☐ Sewing needle & matching thread
- ☐ ¾" (19 mm) Buttons - 5

Size Information

Finished Chest Measurement:
36{40-43½}"/91.5{101.5-110.5} cm

Size Note: We have printed the instructions for the sizes in different colors to make it easier for you to find:

- size Small in Blue
- size Medium in Pink
- size Large in Green

Instructions in Black apply to all sizes.

Gauge Information

With larger size needles,
in Slip Stitch pattern,
13 sts and 28 rows = 4" (10 cm)

Technique Used

- K2 tog ***(Fig. 6, page 46)***

Slip Stitch Pattern

When instructed to slip a stitch, always slip as if to **purl**. On **right** side rows, always hold yarn in **back**.

Row 1 (Right side)**:** With MC, knit across.
Row 2: Knit across.
Note: Carry unused yarn **loosely** along the edge.
Row 3: With CC, K1, (slip 1, K1) across.
Row 4: K1, (WYF slip 1, WYB K1) across.
Row 5: With MC, knit across.
Row 6: Knit across.
Row 7: With CC, K2, slip 1, (K1, slip 1) across to last 2 sts, K2.
Row 8: K2, WYF slip 1, (WYB K1, WYF slip 1) across to last 2 sts, WYB K2.
Repeat Rows 1-8 for Slip Stitch Pattern.

Back

Body

With MC and larger size needles, cast on 61{67-73} sts.

Row 1: Purl across.

Row 2 (Right side)**:** Knit across.

Row 3: Purl across.

Beginning with Row 1 of Slip Stitch Pattern, work until Body measures approximately 11" (28 cm) from bottom of rolled edge, ending by working pattern Row 4.

Armhole Shaping

Rows 1 and 2: With MC, bind off 3 sts at the beginning of the row, knit across: 55{61-67} sts.

Row 3: With CC, K2 tog, K1, (slip 1, K1) across to last 2 sts, K2 tog: 53{59-65} sts.

Row 4: K2, WYF slip 1, (WYB K1, WYF slip 1) across to last 2 sts, K2.

Row 5: With MC, K2 tog, knit across to last 2 sts, K2 tog: 51{57-63} sts.

Row 6: Knit across.

Row 7: With CC, K2 tog, slip 1, (K1, slip 1) across to last 2 sts, K2 tog: 49{55-61} sts.

Beginning with Row 4 of Slip Stitch Pattern, work even until Armholes measure approximately 9½{10-10½}"/24{25.5-26.5} cm, ending by working pattern Row 4 or Row 8; cut CC.

Shoulder Shaping

Note: Maintain established pattern throughout.

Rows 1 and 2: With MC, bind off 5{5-7} sts at the beginning of the row, work across: 39{45-47} sts.

Rows 3-6: Bind off 5{6-6} sts at the beginning of the row, work across: 19{21-23} sts.

With MC, bind off remaining sts.

Left Front

Body

With MC and larger size needles, cast on 29{33-35} sts.

Work same as Back to Armhole Shaping.

Armhole Shaping

Row 1 (Right side)**:** With MC, bind off 3 sts, knit across: 26{30-32} sts.

Row 2: Knit across.

Row 3: With CC, K2 tog, (K1, slip 1) across to last 2 sts, K2: 25{29-31} sts.

Row 4: K2, WYF slip 1, (WYB K1, WYF slip 1) across to last 2 sts, K2.

Row 5: With MC, K2 tog, knit across: 24{28-30} sts.

Row 6: Knit across.

Row 7: With CC, K2 tog, (slip 1, K1) across: 23{27-29} sts.

Rows 8-16: Beginning with Row 4 of Slip Stitch Pattern, work even for 9 rows.

Neck Shaping

Row 1 (Right side - Decrease row)**:** With MC, knit across to last 2 sts, K2 tog: 22{26-28} sts.

Row 2: Knit across.

Row 3: With CC, K2, (slip 1, K1) across.

Row 4: K1, WYF slip 1, (WYB K1, WYF slip 1) across to last 2 sts, K2.

Row 5 (Decrease row)**:** With MC, knit across to last 2 sts, K2 tog: 21{25-27} sts.

Row 6: Knit across.

Row 7: With CC, K1, (slip 1, K1) across.

Row 8: K1, (WYF slip 1, WYB K1) across.

Rows 9 thru 29{37-37}: Repeat Rows 1-8, 2{3-3} times; then repeat Rows 1-5 once **more**: 15{17-19} sts.

Beginning with Row 2 of Slip Stitch Pattern, work even until Armhole measures same as Back to Shoulder Shaping, ending by working pattern Row 4 or Row 8; cut CC.

Shoulder Shaping

Note: Maintain established pattern throughout.

Row 1: With MC, bind off 5{5-7} sts, knit across: 10{12-12} sts.

Row 2: Knit across.

Row 3: With CC, bind off 5{6-6} sts, work across: 5{6-6} sts.

Row 4: Work across.

With MC, bind off remaining sts.

Right Front

Body

With MC and larger size needles, cast on 29{33-35} sts.

Work same as Back to Armhole Shaping.

Armhole Shaping

Row 1 (Right side)**:** With MC, knit across.

Row 2: Bind off 3 sts, knit across: 26{30-32} sts.

Row 3: With CC, K2, (slip 1, K1) across to last 2 sts, K2 tog: 25{29-31} sts.

Row 4: K2, WYF slip 1, (WYB K1, WYF slip 1) across to last 2 sts, K2.

Row 5: With MC, knit across to last 2 sts, K2 tog: 24{28-30} sts.

Row 6: Knit across.

Row 7: With CC, (K1, slip 1) across to last 2 sts, K2 tog: 23{27-29} sts.

Rows 8-16: Beginning with Row 4 of Slip Stitch Pattern, work even for 9 rows.

Neck Shaping

Row 1 (Right side - Decrease row)**:** With MC, K2 tog, knit across: 22{26-28} sts.

Row 2: Knit across.

Row 3: With CC, (K1, slip 1) across to last 2 sts, K2.

Row 4: K2, (WYF slip 1, WYB K1) across.

Row 5 (Decrease row)**:** With MC, K2 tog, knit across: 21{25-27} sts.

Row 6: Knit across.

Row 7: With CC, K1, (slip 1, K1) across.

Row 8: K1, (WYF slip 1, WYB K1) across.

Rows 9 thru 29{37-37}: Repeat Rows 1-8, 2{3-3} times; then repeat Rows 1-5 once **more**: 15{17-19} sts.

Beginning with Row 2 of Slip Stitch Pattern, work even until Armhole measures same as Back to Shoulder Shaping, ending by working pattern Row 4 or Row 8; cut CC.

Shoulder Shaping

Note: Maintain established pattern throughout.

Row 1: With MC, knit across.

Row 2: Bind off 5{5-7} sts, knit across: 10{12-12} sts.

Row 3: With CC, work across.

Row 4: Bind off 5{6-6} sts, work across; cut CC: 5{6-6} sts.

Row 5: With MC, knit across.

Bind off remaining sts.

Finishing

Sew shoulder seams.

Front & Neck Ribbing

With **right** side facing, using MC and circular needle and allowing bottom edge to stay rolled, pick up 52 sts evenly spaced across Right Front to Neck Shaping ***(Figs. 12a & b page 47)***, place marker ***(see Markers page 45)***, pick up 51{55-59} sts evenly spaced across to shoulder seam, pick up 19{21-23} sts across Back neck edge, pick up 51{55-59} sts evenly spaced across Left Front Neck Shaping, pick up 52 sts evenly spaced across to bottom edge: 225{235-245} sts.

Row 1: P1, (K1, P1) across.

Row 2 (Right side)**:** K1, (P1, K1) across.

Row 3 (Buttonhole row)**:** P1, (K1, P1) across to marker, bind off next st in pattern, ★ (K1, P1) 5 times, bind off next st in pattern; repeat from ★ across to last 2 sts, K1, P1.

Row 4: K1, P1, K1, **turn**; add on one st ***(Figs. 5a & b, page 46)***, **turn**; ★ K1, (P1, K1) 5 times, **turn**; add on one st, **turn**; repeat from ★ 3 times **more**, K1, (P1, K1) across.

Row 5: P1, (K1, P1) across.

Bind off all sts in ribbing.

Armhole Ribbing

With **right** side facing, using MC and circular needle, and starting at underarm seam, pick up 70{76-78} sts evenly spaced around armhole edge; place marker to indicate the beginning of rnd ***(see Markers, page 45)***.

Work in K1, P1 ribbing for 1" (2.5 cm).

Bind off all sts in ribbing.

Repeat for second armhole.

Weave side seams ***(Fig. 13, page 47)***.

Sew buttons to Left Front opposite buttonholes.

BACK

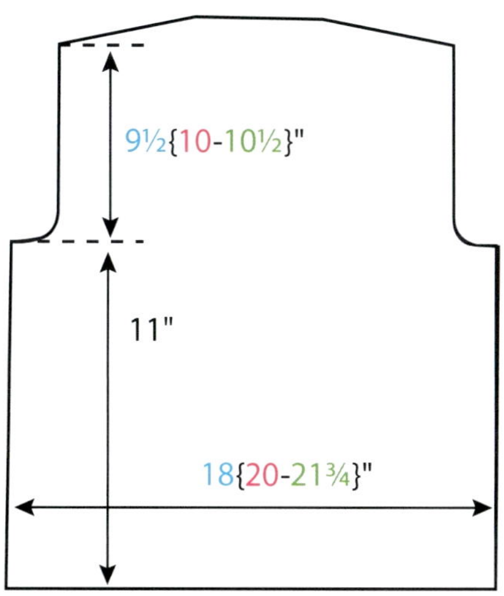

LEFT FRONT

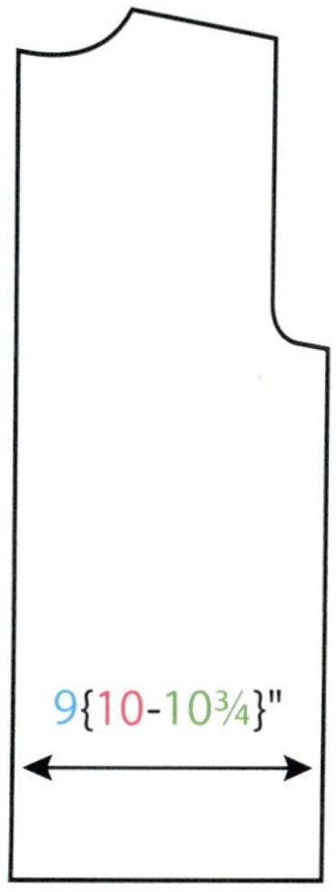

EASY

Cowl Neck Tunic

Shopping List

Yarn (Bulky Weight) BULKY 5
[6 ounces, 185 yards
(170 grams, 169 meters) per skein]:
☐ {4-5}{5-5-6} skeins

Knitting Needles
Straight,
☐ Size 10½ (6.5 mm) **or** size needed for gauge
16" (40.5 cm) Circular,
☐ Size 9 (5.5 mm) **and**
☐ Size 10 (6 mm)

Additional Supplies
☐ Stitch holder
☐ Marker
☐ Yarn needle

Size Information

Finished Chest Measurement:
{36-38½}{40-42½-45}"/
{91.5-98}{101.5-108-114.5} cm

Size Note: We have printed the instructions for the sizes in different colors to make it easier for you to find:

- size Small in Blue
- size Medium in Pink
- size Large in Green
- size 1X in Purple
- size 2X in Red

Instructions in Black apply to all sizes.

Gauge Information

With larger size needles,
in Stockinette Stitch
(knit one row, purl one row),
13 sts and 17 rows = 4" (10 cm)

Techniques Used

- Increases ***(pages 45 & 46)***
- K2 tog ***(Fig. 6, page 46)***
- Slip 1, K1, PSSO ***(Figs. 8a & b, pages 46 & 47)***
- P2 tog ***(Fig. 10, page 47)***
- P2 tog tbl ***(Fig. 11, page 47)***

Back
Body
With larger size needles, cast on {61-65}{67-71-75} sts.

Rows 1-5: Beginning with a **purl** row, work in Stockinette Stitch.

Row 6 (Right side)**:** K1, (P1, K1) across.

Rows 7 and 8: P1, (K1, P1) across.

Rows 9 and 10: K1, (P1, K1) across.

Repeat Rows 7-10 for pattern until piece measures approximately 8" (20.5 cm) from bottom of rolled edge, ending by working Row 7 or Row 9.

Beginning with a **knit** row, work in Stockinette Stitch until Body measures approximately {23½-23½}{24½-24½-25½}"/(59.5-59.5}{62-62-65} cm from bottom of rolled edge, ending by working a **purl** row.

Shoulder Shaping
Note: Maintain established pattern throughout.

Rows 1-4: Bind off {5-6}{6-7-8} sts at the beginning of the row, work across: {41-41}{43-43-43} sts.

Rows 5 and 6: Bind off {6-6}{7-7-7} sts at the beginning of the row, work across: 29 sts.

Bind off remaining sts.

Front
Body
Work same as Back until Front measures approximately {20-20}{21-21-22}"/{51-51}{53.5-53.5-56} cm from bottom of rolled edge, ending by working a **knit** row.

Neck Shaping
Note: Both sides of Neck are worked at the same time, using separate yarn for **each** side.

Row 1: Purl {22-24}{25-27-29} sts, slip next 17 sts onto st holder; with second yarn, purl across: {22-24}{25-27-29} sts **each** side.

Row 2: Knit across to within 2 sts of Neck edge, K2 tog; with second yarn, slip 1 as if to **knit**, K1, PSSO, knit across: {21-23}{24-26-28} sts **each** side.

Row 3: Purl across to within 2 sts of Neck edge, P2 tog tbl; with second yarn, P2 tog, purl across: {20-22}{23-25-27} sts **each** side.

Row 4 (Decrease row)**:** Knit across to within 2 sts of Neck edge, K2 tog; with second yarn, slip 1 as if to **knit**, K1, PSSO, knit across: {19-21}{22-24-26} sts **each** side.

Row 5: Purl across; with second yarn, purl across.

Rows 6-10: Repeat Rows 4 and 5 twice, then repeat Row 4 once **more**: {16-18}{19-21-23} sts **each** side.

Work even until Front measures same as Back to Shoulder Shaping, ending by working a **purl** row.

Shoulder Shaping
Rows 1-4: Bind off {5-6}{6-7-8} sts at Armhole edge, work across; with second yarn, work across: {6-6}{7-7-7} sts **each** side.

Row 5: Bind off remaining sts on first side; with second yarn, knit across.

Bind off remaining sts.

Sleeve (Make 2)
Body
With larger size needles, cast on {31-31}{33-33-35} sts.

Rows 1-4: Beginning with a **purl** row, work in Stockinette Stitch.

Row 5: Purl across increasing 8 sts evenly spaced: {39-39}{41-41-43} sts.

Row 6 (Right side)**:** K1, (P1, K1) across.

Rows 7 and 8: P1, (K1, P1) across.

Rows 9 and 10: K1, (P1, K1) across.

Repeat Rows 7-10 for pattern until piece measures approximately 6" (15 cm) from bottom of rolled edge, ending by working Row 7 or Row 9.

Beginning with a **knit** row, work in Stockinette Stitch increasing one stitch at **each** edge, every other row, {0-0}{0-3-4} times ***(see Zeros, page 45)***; then increase every fourth row, {5-10}{9-9-9} times; then increase every sixth row, {3-0}{1-0-0} time(s): {55-59}{61-65-69} sts.

Work even until Sleeve measures approximately {17-17½}{18-18-18½}"/{43-44.5}{45.5-45.5-47} cm from bottom of rolled edge, ending by working a **purl** row.

Bind off all sts in **knit**.

Finishing

Sew shoulder seams.

Cowl Neck

With **right** side facing and using smaller size circular needle, pick up 15 sts evenly spaced along left Front Neck edge ***(Figs. 12a & b, page 47)***, knit 17 sts from Front st holder, pick up 15 sts evenly spaced along right Front Neck edge, pick up 29 sts across Back Neck edge, place marker to indicate the beginning of rnd ***(see Markers, page 45)***: 76 sts.

Rnds 1 and 2: (P1, K1) around.

Rnds 3 and 4: (K1, P1) around.

Repeat Rnds 1-4 until Cowl measures approximately 3" (7.5 cm), ending by working Rnd 4.

Change to larger size circular needle.

Repeat Rnds 1-4 until Cowl measures approximately 6" (15 cm), ending by working Rnd 4.

Purl every rnd for 1" (2.5 cm).

Bind off all sts **loosely** in **purl**.

Turn Cowl Neck to **right** side allowing edges to roll.

Sew Sleeves to Tunic matching center of last row on Sleeve to shoulder seam and beginning {8½-9}{9½-10-10½}"/{21.5-23}{24-25.5-26.5} cm down from seam.

Weave underarm and side in one continuous seam ***(Fig. 13, page 47)***.

BACK

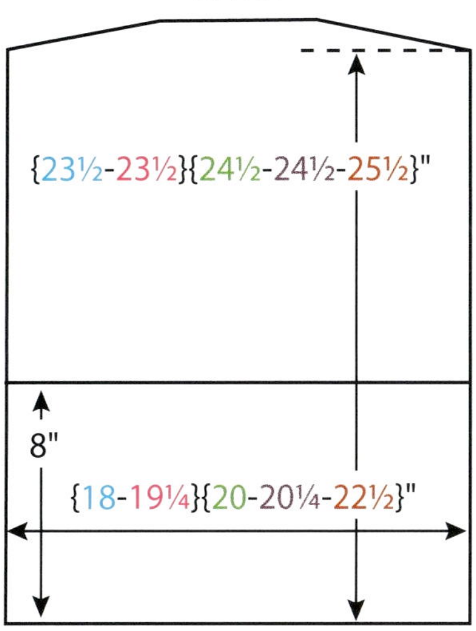

FRONT

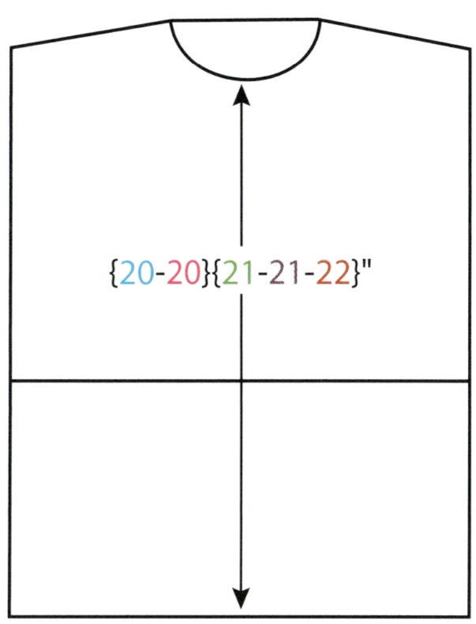

SLEEVE

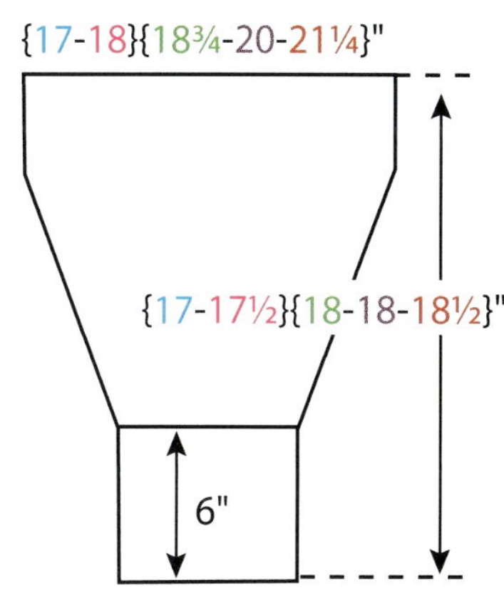

EASY

Rugby Pullover

Shopping List

Yarn (Bulky Weight) 5 BULKY
[6 ounces, 185 yards
(170 grams, 169 meters) per skein]:
- ☐ MC (Tan) - {3-3}{3-3-4} skeins
- ☐ CC (Blue) - {2-2}{2-2-3} skeins

Knitting Needles
Straight,
- ☐ Size 10½ (6.5 mm) **or** size needed for gauge

24" (61 cm) Circular,
- ☐ Size 8 (5 mm)

Additional Supplies
- ☐ Stitch holder
- ☐ Marker
- ☐ Yarn needle
- ☐ Sewing needle & matching thread
- ☐ ¾" (19 mm) Buttons - 2

Size Information

Finished Chest Measurement:
{38-40½}{42-44-46½}"/
{96.5-103}{106.5-112-118} cm

Size Note: We have printed the instructions for the sizes in different colors to make it easier for you to find:

- size Small in Blue
- size Medium in Pink
- size Large in Green
- size 1X in Purple
- size 2X in Red

Instructions in Black apply to all sizes.

Gauge Information

With larger size needles,
in Stockinette Stitch
(knit one row, purl one row),
13 sts and 17 rows = 4" (10 cm)

Techniques Used

- Increases ***(pages 45 & 46)***
- K2 tog ***(Fig. 6, page 46)***
- Slip 1, K1, PSSO ***(Figs. 8a & b, pages 46 & 47)***
- P2 tog ***(Fig. 10, page 47)***
- P2 tog tbl ***(Fig. 11, page 47)***

Color Sequence

★ 10 rows MC, 4 rows CC, 2 rows MC, 4 rows CC; repeat from ★ for sequence.

Back

With MC and larger size needles, cast on {64-68}{70-74-78} sts.

Note: Follow Color Sequence throughout.

Beginning with a **purl** row, work in Stockinette Stitch until Back measures approximately {20-20}{20½-21-22}"/{51-51}{52-53.5-56} cm from bottom of rolled edge, ending by working a **purl** row.

Neck & Shoulder Shaping

Rows 1-4: Bind off {4-5}{5-5-6} sts at the beginning of the row, work across: {48-48}{50-54-54} sts.

Note: Both sides of Neck are worked at the same time, using separate yarn for **each** side.

Row 5: Bind off {5-5}{5-6-6} sts, knit {5-5}{5-6-6} sts, slip next {26-26}{28-28-28} sts onto st holder; with second yarn, knit across.

Row 6: Bind off {5-5}{5-6-6} sts at Armhole edge, purl across to within 2 sts of neck edge, P2 tog tbl; with second yam, P2 tog, purl across: {5-5}{5-6-6} sts **each** side.

Row 7: Bind off sts on first side; with second yarn, knit across.

Bind off remaining sts in **purl**.

Front

Work same as Back until Front measures approximately {13-13}{13-13½-14½}"/{33-33}{33-34.5-37} cm from bottom of rolled edge, ending by working a **purl** row.

Placket Opening

Note: Both sides of Placket Opening are worked at the same time, using separate yarn for **each** side.

Row 1: Knit {29-31}{32-34-36} sts; with second yarn, bind off next 6 sts, knit across: {29-31}{32-34-36} sts **each** side.

Work even until Placket Opening measures approximately 4¼" (11 cm), ending by working a **purl** row.

Neck Shaping

Note: Maintain established pattern throughout.

Rows 1-4: Work across; with second yarn, bind off 3 sts at Neck edge, work across: {23-25}{26-28-30} sts **each** side.

Row 5: Knit across to within 2 sts of Neck edge, K2 tog; with second yarn, slip 1 as if to **knit**, K1, PSSO, knit across: {22-24}{25-27-29} sts **each** side.

Row 6: Purl across to within 2 sts of Neck edge, P2 tog tbl; with second yam, P2 tog, purl across: {21-23}{24-26-28} sts.

Row 7 (Decrease row)**:** Knit across to within 2 sts of Neck edge, K2 tog; with second yarn, slip 1 as if to **knit**, K1, PSSO, knit across: {20-22}{23-25-27} sts **each** side.

Row 8: Purl across; with second yarn, purl across.

Repeat Rows 7 and 8, {2-2}{3-3-3} times: {18-20}{20-22-24} sts **each** side.

Shoulder Shaping

Rows 1-4: Bind off {4-5}{5-5-6} sts at Armhole edge, work across; with second yarn, work across: {10-10}{10-12-12} sts **each** side.

Rows 5 and 6: Bind off {5-5}{5-6-6} sts at Armhole edge, work across; with second yarn, work across: {5-5}{5-6-6} sts **each** side.

Row 7: Bind off remaining sts on first side; with second yarn, knit across.

Bind off remaining sts.

Sleeve (Make 2)

With MC and larger size needles, cast on {26-28}{28-30-30} sts.

Note: Follow Color Sequence throughout.

Beginning with a **purl** row, work in Stockinette Stitch until Sleeve measures approximately 2" (5 cm) from bottom of rolled edge, ending by working a **purl** row.

Beginning with the next row, knit increase one stitch at **each** edge, every other row, {2-1}{5-6-7} time(s); then knit increase every fourth row, {13-14}{12-12-12} times: {56-58}{62-66-68} sts.

Work even until Sleeve measures approximately {17-17½}{17½-18-18½}"/ {43-44.5}{44.5-45.5-47} cm from bottom of rolled edge, ending by working a **purl** row.

Bind off all sts in **knit**.

Finishing

Sew shoulder seams.

Sew Sleeves to Sweater, matching center of last row on Sleeve to shoulder seam and beginning {8½-9}{9½-10-10½}"/{21.5-23} {24-25.5-26.5} cm down from seam.

Weave underarm and side in one continuous seam ***(Fig. 13, page 47)***.

Neck Band

Note: To pick up and knit stitches, pick up a stitch ***(Figs. 12a & b, page 47)***, place it on the left needle and knit the stitch.

With **right** side facing, using CC and circular needle, pick up and knit 18 sts evenly spaced along right Neck edge, slip {26-26}{28-28-28} sts from Back st holder onto second end of circular needle and knit across, pick up and knit 18 sts along left Neck edge: {62-62}{64-64-64} sts.

Note: Rather than making the Neck Band separately and then sewing it to the neckline, you will work in short rows, which are rows that are not worked all the way from one end to the other. The first row is worked across the left neck and the Back, and only 3 stitches on the right neck. Leaving the remaining stitches unworked, you will stop, **turn** the work, and work the next row in the opposite direction. For each of the remaining rows you will work across 3 **more** stitches until all of the stitches are on the same needle. Work in short rows as follows:

Row 1: K1, (P1, K1) across: {47-47}{49-49-49} sts, **turn**.

Row 2: Work across {32-32}{34-34-34} sts in Seed St (knit the purl stitches and purl the knit stitches as they face you), **turn**.

Note: Maintain established pattern throughout.

Row 3: Work across {35-35}{37-37-37} sts, **turn**.

Row 4: Work across {38-38}{40-40-40} sts, **turn**.

Row 5: Work across {41-41}{43-43-43} sts, **turn**.

Row 6: Work across {44-44}{46-46-46} sts, **turn**.

Row 7: Work across {47-47}{49-49-49} sts, **turn**.

Row 8: Work across {50-50}{52-52-52} sts, **turn**.

Row 9: Work across {53-53}{55-55-55} sts, **turn**.

Row 10: Work across {56-56}{58-58-58} sts, **turn**.

Row 11: Work across, **turn**.

Row 12: Work across; do **not** turn: {62-62}{64-64-64} sts.

Front Placket

Row 1: Pick up and knit 14 sts evenly spaced along left Front Placket Opening, **turn**; work across, pick up and knit 14 sts evenly spaced along right Front Placket Opening: {90-90}{92-92-92} sts.

Row 2: Work across.

Place first marker in stitch 2" (5 cm) from bottom edge of Placket on right Front, and second marker 2" (5 cm) up from first marker.

Row 3 (Buttonhole row)**:** (Work across to marker, bind off next 2 sts) twice, work across.

Row 4: ★ Work across to bound off sts; **turn**, add on 2 sts ***(Figs. 5a & b, page 46)***; **turn**; repeat from ★ once **more**, work across.

Row 5: Work across.

Bind off all sts in pattern.

Sew buttons opposite buttonholes.

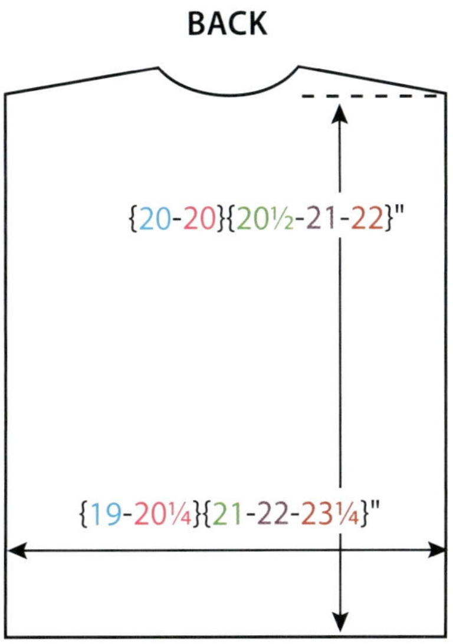

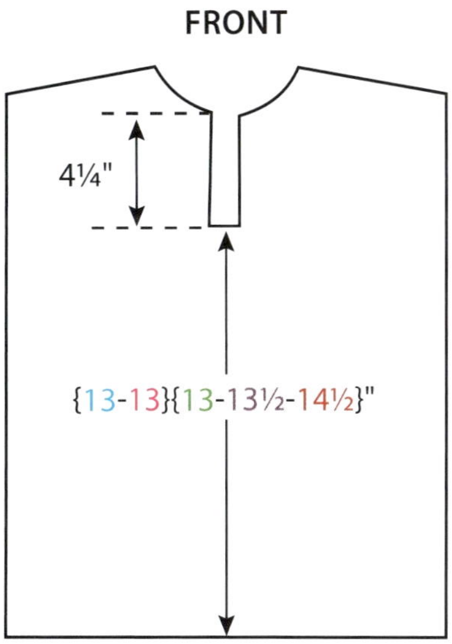

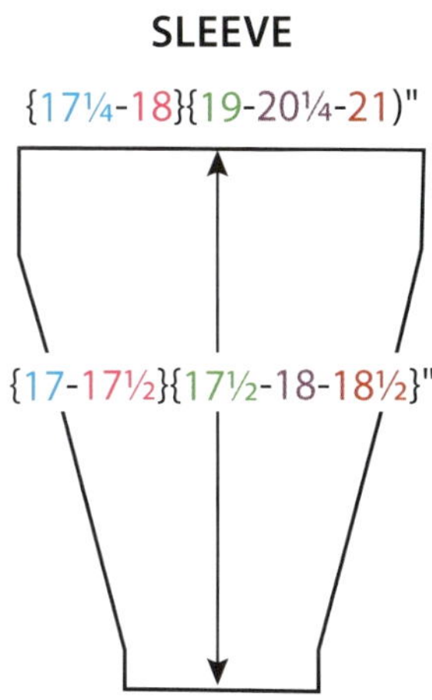

EASY

Scoop Neck Pullover

Shopping List

Yarn (Bulky Weight) BULKY 5
[6 ounces, 185 yards
(170 grams, 169 meters) per skein]:
- ☐ {4-5}{5-5-6} skeins

Knitting Needles
Straight,
- ☐ Size 10½ (6.5 mm) **or** size needed for gauge

16" (40.5 cm) Circular,
- ☐ Size 9 (5.5 mm)

Additional Supplies
- ☐ Stitch holder - 2
- ☐ Marker
- ☐ Yarn needle

Size Information

Finished Chest Measurement:
{35-37½}{40-42½-45}"/
{89-95.5}{101.5-108-114.5} cm

Size Note: We have printed the instructions for the sizes in different colors to make it easier for you to find:

- size Small in Blue
- size Medium in Pink
- size Large in Green
- size 1X in Purple
- size 2X in Red

Instructions in Black apply to all sizes.

Gauge Information

With larger size needles,
in Stockinette Stitch
(knit one row, purl one row),
13 sts and 17 rows = 4" (10 cm)

Techniques Used

- Increases ***(pages 45 & 46)***
- K2 tog ***(Fig. 6, page 46)***
- Slip 1, K1, PSSO ***(Figs. 8a & b, pages 46 & 47)***
- P2 tog ***(Fig. 10, page 47)***
- P2 tog tbl ***(Fig. 11, page 46)***

Front

Work same as Back through Row 8 of Armhole Shaping: {47-51}{53-57-61} sts.

Neck Shaping

Note: Both sides of Neck are worked at the same time, using separate yarn for **each** side.

Row 1: Knit {21-23}{24-26-28} sts, slip next 5 sts onto st holder; with second yarn, knit across: {21-23}{24-26-28} sts **each** side.

Row 2: Purl across; with second yarn, purl across.

Row 3 (Decrease row)**:** Knit across to within 2 sts of Neck edge, K2 tog; with second yarn, slip 1 as if to **knit**, K1, PSSO, knit across: {20-22}{23-25-27} sts **each** side.

Rows 4-21: Repeat Rows 2 and 3, 9 times: {11-13}{14-16-18} sts **each** side.

Work even until Armholes measure same as Back to Shoulder Shaping, ending by working a **purl** row.

Shoulder Shaping

Rows 1 and 2: Bind off {3-4}{4-5-6} sts at Armhole edge, work across; with second yarn, work across: {8-9}{10-11-12} sts **each** side.

Rows 3 and 4: Bind off {4-4}{5-5-6} sts at Armhole edge, work across; with second yarn, work across: {4-5}{5-6-6} sts **each** side.

Row 5: Bind off remaining sts on first side; with second yarn, work across.

Bind off remaining sts.

Back

With larger size needles, cast on {59-63}{67-71-75} sts.

Beginning with a **purl** row, work in Stockinette Stitch until Back measures approximately {12-12}{13-13-14}"/{30.5-30.5}{33-33-35.5} cm from bottom of rolled edge, ending by working a **purl** row.

Armhole Shaping

Rows 1 and 2: Bind off {3-3}{4-4-4} sts at the beginning of the next row, work across: {53-57}{59-63-67} sts.

Row 3 (Decrease row)**:** K1, slip 1 as if to **knit**, K1, PSSO, knit across to last 3 sts, K2 tog, K1: {51-55}{57-61-65} sts.

Row 4: Purl across.

Rows 5-7: Repeat Rows 3 and 4 once, then repeat Row 3 once **more**: {47-51}{53-57-61} sts.

Work even until Armholes measure approximately {8½-8½}{9-9½-10}"/{21.5-21.5}{23-24-25.5} cm, ending by working a **purl** row.

Neck & Shoulder Shaping

Note: Both sides of Neck are worked at the same time, using a separate yarn for **each** side.

Row 1: Bind off {3-4}{4-5-6} sts, knit {8-9}{10-11-12} sts, slip next 23 sts onto st holder; with second yarn, knit across.

Row 2: Bind off {3-4}{4-5-6} sts, purl across to within 2 sts of Neck edge, P2 tog tbl; with second yarn, P2 tog, purl across: {8-9}{10-11-12} sts **each** side.

Rows 3 and 4: Bind off {4-4}{5-5-6} sts at Armhole edge, work across; with second yarn, work across: {4-5}{5-6-6} sts **each** side.

Row 5: Bind off remaining sts on first side; with second yarn, work across.

Bind off remaining sts.

Sleeve (Make 2)

Ribbing

With larger size needles, cast on {26-26}{28-28-30} sts.

Work in K1, P1 ribbing for 1½" (4 cm).

Body

Row 1: Knit across increasing 8 sts evenly spaced: {34-34}{36-36-38} sts.

Beginning with a **purl** row, work in Stockinette Stitch increasing one stitch at **each** edge, every eighth row, {0-0}{0-4-3} times ***(see Zeros, page 45)***; then increase every tenth row, {5-6}{6-3-4} times: {44-46}{48-50-52} sts.

Work even until Sleeve measures approximately {17½-17½}{18-18-18½}"/{44.5-44.5}{45.5-45.5-47} cm from cast on edge, ending by working a **purl** row.

Sleeve Cap

Rows 1 and 2: Bind off {3-3}{4-4-4} sts at the beginning of the row, work across: {38-40}{40-42-44} sts.

Row 3 (Decrease row): K1, slip 1 as if to **knit**, K1, PSSO, knit across to last 3 sts, K2 tog, K1: {36-38}{38-40-42} sts.

Row 4: Purl across.

Rows 5-7: Repeat Rows 3 and 4 once, then repeat Row 3 once **more**: {32-34}{34-36-38} sts.

Work even until Sleeve Cap measures approximately {6-6}{6½-6½-6½}"/{15-15}{16.5-16.5-16.5} cm, ending by working a **purl** row.

Next 2 Rows: Bind off {11-11}{11-12-13} sts at the beginning of the row, work across: {10-12}{12-12-12} sts.

Bind off remaining sts.

Finishing

Sew shoulder seams.

Neck Edging

With **right** side facing, slip 23 sts from Back st holder onto circular needle and knit across, pick up {36-36}{38-40-42} sts along left Neck edge ***(Fig. 12a, page 47)***, slip 5 sts from Front st holder onto second end of circular needle and knit across, pick up {36-36}{38-40-42} sts along right Neck edge, place marker to indicate the beginning of rnd ***(see Markers, page 45)***: {100-100}{104-108-112} sts.

Knit around for 2½" (6.5 cm).

Bind off all sts.

Set in Sleeves, matching center of Sleeve Cap to shoulder seam.

Weave underarm and side in one continuous seam ***(Fig. 13, page 47)***.

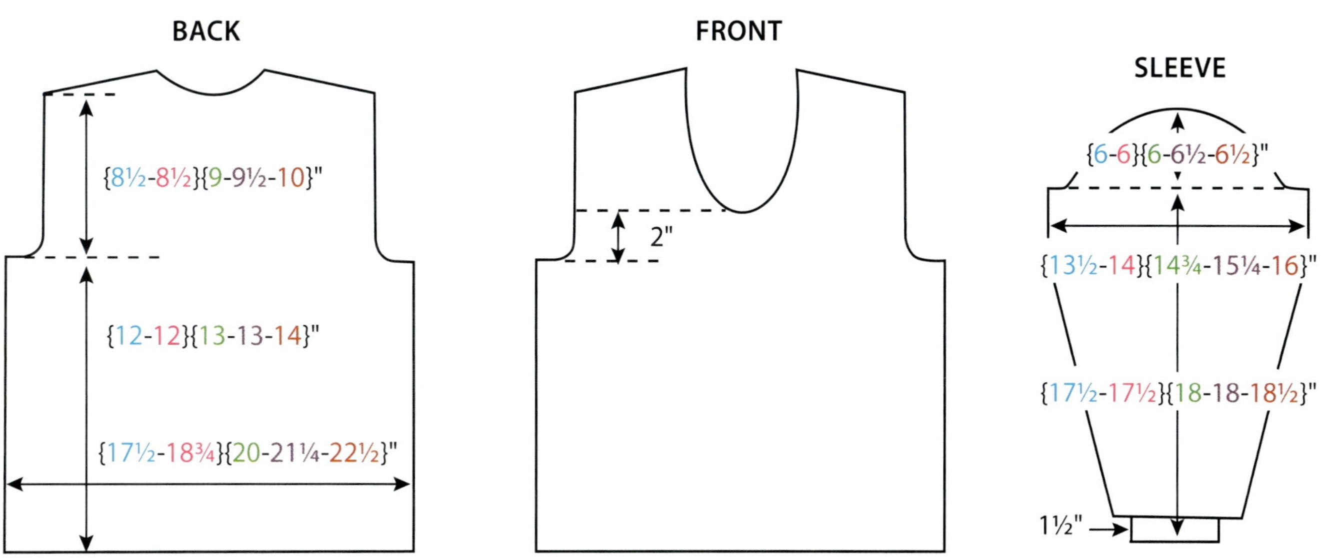

EASY

Lacy Pullover

Shopping List

Yarn (Bulky Weight) BULKY 5
[6 ounces, 185 yards
(170 grams, 169 meters) per skein]:
- ☐ 4{5-6} skeins

Knitting Needles
Straight,
- ☐ Size 8 (5 mm) **and**
- ☐ Size 10 (6 mm) **or**
sizes needed for gauge

16" (40.5 mm) Circular,
- ☐ Size 8 (5 mm)

Additional Supplies
- ☐ Stitch holders - 2
- ☐ Marker
- ☐ Yarn needle

Size Information

Finished Chest Measurement:
37½{45-52½}"/95.5{114.5-133.5} cm

Size Note: We have printed the instructions for the sizes in different colors to make it easier for you to find:

- size Small in Blue
- size Medium in Pink
- size Large in Green

Instructions in Black apply to all sizes.

Gauge Information

With larger size needles,
in pattern, 12 sts
(one pattern repeat) = 3¾" (9.5 cm)
With larger size needles,
in Stockinette Stitch
(knit one row, purl one row),
13 sts and 17 rows = 4" (10 cm)

Techniques Used

- Increasing Evenly Spaced ***(page 45)***
- Purl increase ***(Fig. 3, page 46)***
- YO ***(Fig. 4, page 46)***
- K2 tog ***(Fig. 6, page 46)***
- K4 tog ***(Fig. 7, page 46)***
- Slip 1, K1, PSSO ***(Figs. 8a & b, pages 46 & 47)***
- Slip 1, K2 tog, PSSO ***(Fig. 9, page 47)***

Heart Pattern

Row 1 (Right side): K6, YO, K1, YO, K6.

Row 2 AND ALL WRONG SIDE ROWS: Purl across.

Row 3: K2, YO, K4 tog, YO, K3, YO, K4 tog, YO, K2.

Row 5: K2, K2 tog, YO, K5, YO, slip 1 as if to **knit**, K1, PSSO, K2.

Row 7: K1, K2 tog, YO, K7, YO, skip 1 as if to **knit**, K1, PSSO, K1.

Row 9: K2 tog, YO, K9, YO, slip 1 as if to **knit**, K1, PSSO.

Row 10: Purl across.

Repeat Rows 1-10 for Heart Pattern.

Back

Ribbing

With smaller size straight needles, cast on 62{74-86} sts.

Row 1: P2, (K2, P2) across.

Row 2 (Right side)**:** K2, (P2, K2) across.

Repeat Rows 1 and 2 until Ribbing measures approximate!y 2" (5 cm), ending by working Row 2.

Body

Change to larger size needles.

Row 1: Purl increase, purl across: 63{75-87} sts.

Row 2 (Right side)**:** K2, YO, K2 tog, K3, YO, K1, YO, K3, slip 1 as if to **knit**, K1, PSSO, ★ YO, K1, YO, K2 tog, K3, YO, K1, YO, K3, slip 1 as if to **knit**, K1, PSSO; repeat from ★ across to last 2 sts, YO, K2.

Row 3 AND ALL WRONG SIDE ROWS: Purl across.

Row 4: K3,★ YO, K4 tog, YO, K3; repeat from ★ across.

Row 6: K3,★ K2 tog, YO, K5, YO, slip 1 as if to **knit**, K1, PSSO, K3; repeat from ★ across.

Row 8: K2, K2 tog, YO, K7, YO, slip 1 as if to **knit**, K1, PSSO, ★ K1, K2 tog, YO, K7, YO, slip 1 as if to **knit**, K1, PSSO; repeat from ★ across to last 2 sts, K2.

Row 10: K1, K2 tog, YO, K9, ★ YO, slip 1 as if to **knit**, K2 tog, PSSO, YO, K9; repeat from ★ across to last 3 sts, YO, slip 1 as if to **knit**, K1, PSSO, K1.

Row 11: Purl across.

Repeat Rows 2-11 for pattern until Back measures approximately 22{24¼-24¼}"/56{61.5-61.5} cm from cast on edge, ending by working Row 5.

Shoulder Shaping

Note: Work in Stockinette Stitch throughout.

Rows 1 and 2: Bind off 8{11-14} sts at the beginning of the row, work across: 47{53-59} sts.

Rows 3 and 4: Bind off 9{11-14} sts at the beginning of the row, work across: 29{31-31} sts.

Place remaining sts onto st holder.

Front
Work same as Back.

Sleeve (Make 2)
Ribbing
With smaller size straight needles, cast on 30 sts.

Row 1: P2, (K2, P2) across.

Row 2 (Right side)**:** K2, (P2, K2) across.

Repeat Rows 1 and 2 until Ribbing measures approximately 1½" (4 cm), ending by working Row 2.

Body
Change to larger size needles.

Row 1: Purl across increasing 5{7-9} sts evenly spaced: 35{37-39} sts.

Row 2: K 11{12-13}, place marker *(see Markers, page 45)*, work Row 1 of Heart Pattern, place marker, K 11{12-13}.

Working Heart Pattern between markers and Stockinette Stitch on each side, increase one stitch at **each** edge, every fourth row, 1{6-14} time(s); then increase every sixth row, 9{6-1} time(s): 55{61-69} sts.

Work even until Sleeve measures approximately 17{17½-18}"/43{44.5-45.5} cm from cast on edge, ending by working a **purl** row.

Bind off all sts in **knit**.

Finishing

Sew shoulder seams.

Neck Ribbing

With **right** side facing, slip 29{31-31} sts from Front st holder onto circular needle and knit across, pick up one st at shoulder seam ***(Fig. 12b, page 47)***, slip 29{31-31} sts from Back st holder onto second end of circular needle and knit across, pick up one st at shoulder seam, place marker to indicate the beginning of rnd: 60{64-64} sts.

Work in K2, P2 ribbing around for 2" (5 cm).

Bind off all sts **loosely** in ribbing.

Sew Sleeves to Sweater, matching center of last row on Sleeve to shoulder seam and beginning 8½{9½-10½}"/21.5{24-26.5} cm down from seam.

Weave underarm and side in one continuous seam ***(Fig. 13, page 47)***.

FRONT & BACK

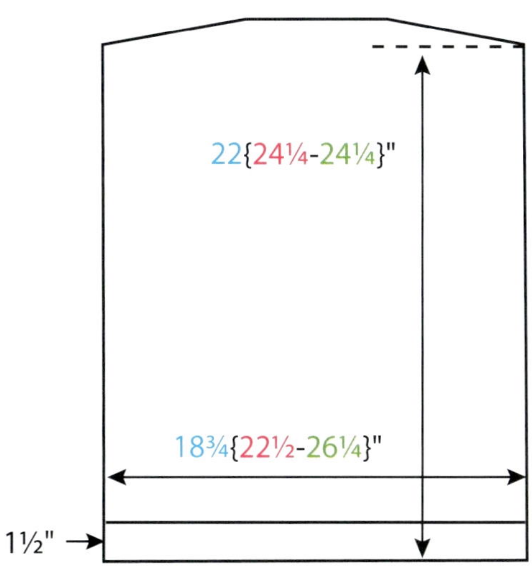

SLEEVE

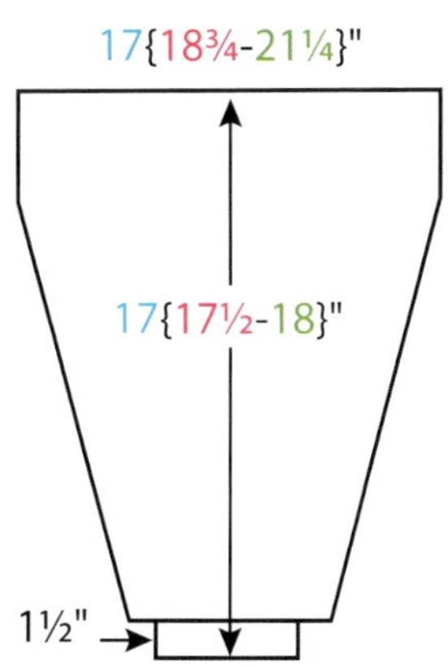

EASY

Ribbed Pullover
Solid Version

Shopping List

Yarn (Bulky Weight) BULKY 5
[6 ounces, 185 yards
(170 grams, 169 meters) per skein]:
☐ {5-5}{5-6-6} skeins

Knitting Needles
Straight,
☐ Size 10½ (6.5 mm) **or** size needed for gauge
16" (40.5 cm) Circular,
☐ Size 9 (5.5 mm)

Additional Supplies
☐ Stitch holder - 2
☐ Marker
☐ Yarn needle

Size Information
Finished Chest Measurement:
{38-40}{42-44-46}"/
{96.5-101.5}{106.5-112-117} cm

Size Note: We have printed the instructions for the sizes in different colors to make it easier for you to find:

- size Small in Blue
- size Medium in Pink
- size Large in Green
- size 1X in Purple
- size 2X in Red

Instructions in Black apply to all sizes.

Gauge Information
With larger size needles,
in ribbed pattern (Rows 5 & 6),
16 sts and 16 rows = 4" (10 cm)

Techniques Used
- Increasing Evenly Spaced *(page 45)*
- Increases *(pages 45 & 46)*
- Decreases *(pages 46 & 47)*
-

Back

With larger size needles, cast on {78-82}{86-90-94} sts.

Rows 1-4: Beginning with a **purl** row, work in Stockinette Stitch.

Row 5: P2, (K2, P2) across.

Row 6 (Right side)**:** K2, (P2, K2) across.

Repeat Rows 5 and 6 for ribbed pattern until Back measures approximately {22-22½}{23-24-24½}"/{56-57}{58.5-61-62} cm from bottom of rolled edge, ending by working Row 5.

Shoulder Shaping

Note: Maintain established pattern throughout.

Rows 1-4: Bind off {9-9}{10-10-11} sts at the beginning of the row, work across: {42-46}{46-50-50} sts.

Rows 5 and 6: Bind off {8-10}{9-11-11} sts at the beginning of the row, work across: {26-26}{28-28-28} sts.

Slip remaining sts onto st holder.

Front

Work same as Back until Front measures approximately {19-19½}{20-21-21½}"/{48.5-49.5}{51-53.5-54.5} cm from bottom of rolled edge, ending by working Row 5.

Neck Shaping

Note: Both sides of Neck are worked at the same time, using separate yarn for **each** side. Maintain established pattern throughout.

Row 1: Work across {32-34}{35-37-39} sts, slip next {14-14}{16-16-16} sts onto st holder; with second yarn, work across: {32-34}{35-37-39} sts **each** side.

Row 2: Work across to within 2 sts of Neck edge, decrease; with second yarn, decrease, work across: {31-33}{34-36-38} sts **each** side.

Row 3 (Decrease row)**:** Work across to within 2 sts of Neck edge, decrease; with second yarn, decrease, work across: {30-32}{33-35-37} sts **each** side.

Row 4: Work across; with second yarn, work across.

Rows 5-12: Repeat Rows 3 and 4, 4 times: {26-28}{29-31-33} sts **each** side.

Shoulder Shaping

Rows 1-4: Bind off {9-9}{10-10-11} sts at Armhole edge work across; with second yarn, work across: {8-10}{9-11-11} sts **each** side.

Row 5: Bind off remaining sts on first side; with second yarn, work across.

Bind off remaining sts.

Sleeve (Make 2)

With larger size needles, cast on 30 sts.

Rows 1-4: Beginning with a **purl** row, work in Stockinette Stitch.

Row 5: Purl across increasing 6 sts evenly spaced: 36 sts.

Rows 6 and 7: (K2, P2) across.

Beginning with the next row and working new stitches in ribbed pattern, increase one stitch at **each** edge, every other row, {3-6}{10-13-16} times; then increase every fourth row, {13-12}{10-9-8} times: {68-72}{76-80-84} sts.

Work even until Sleeve measures approximately {17-17½}{17½-18-18½}"/{43-44.5}{44.5-45.5-47} cm from bottom of rolled edge.

Bind off all sts in pattern.

Finishing

Sew shoulder seams.

Neck Edging

With **right** side facing, slip {26-26}{28-28-28} sts from Back st holder onto circular needle and knit across, pick up 16 sts evenly spaced along left Front Neck edge ***(Fig. 12b, page 47)***, slip {14-14}{16-16-16} sts from Front st holder onto second end of circular needle and knit across, pick up 16 sts evenly spaced along right Front Neck edge, place marker to indicate the beginning of rnd ***(see Markers, page 45)***: {72-72}{76-76-76} sts.

Knit 7 rnds.

Bind off all sts **loosely** in **knit**.

Sew Sleeves to Sweater, matching center of last row on Sleeve to shoulder seam and beginning {8½-9}{9½-10-10½}"/{21.5-23}{24-25.5-26.5} cm down from seam.

Weave underarm and side in one continuous seam ***(Fig. 13, page 47)***.

BACK

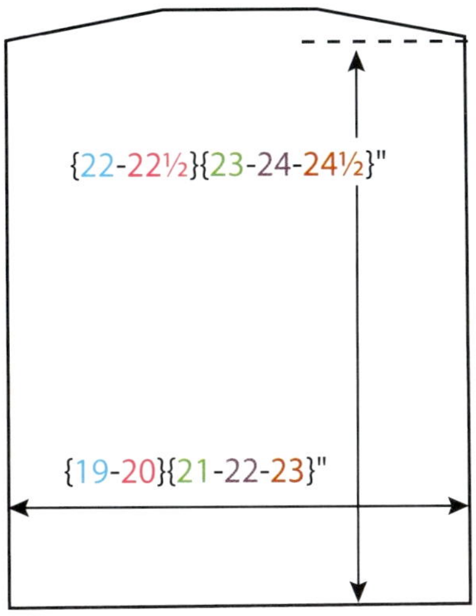

FRONT

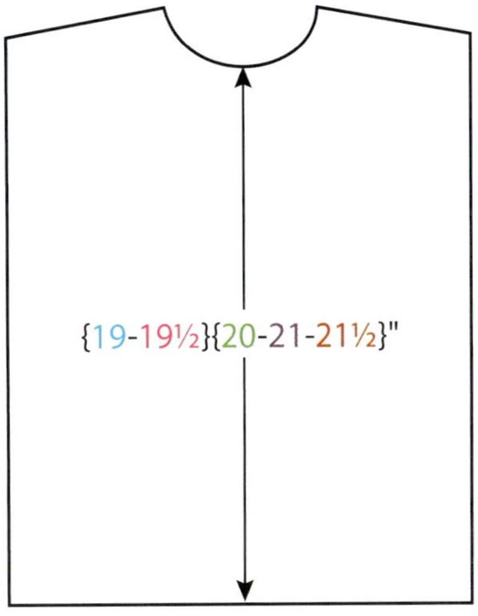

SLEEVE

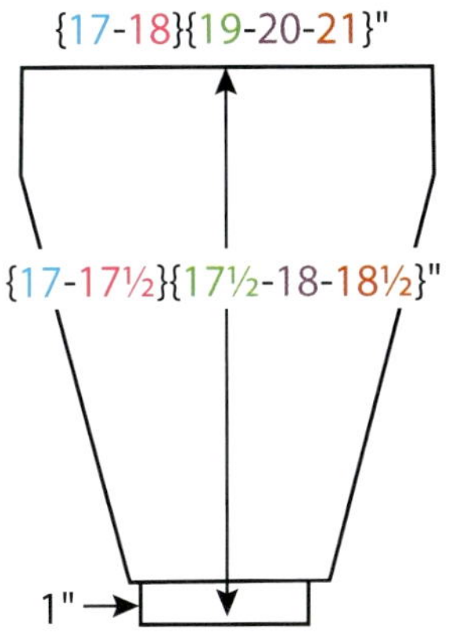

EASY

Ribbed Pullover
Striped Version

Shopping List

Yarn (Bulky Weight) 5 BULKY
[6 ounces, 185 yards
(170 grams, 169 meters) per skein]:
- ☐ Color A (Brown) - 2 skeins
- ☐ Color B (Variegated) - 2 skeins
- ☐ Color C (Off White) - 2 skeins

Knitting Needles
Straight,
- ☐ Size 10½ (6.5 mm) **or** size needed for gauge

16" (40.5 cm) Circular,
- ☐ Size 9 (5.5 mm)

Additional Supplies
- ☐ Stitch holders - 2
- ☐ Marker
- ☐ Yarn needle

Size Information

Finished Chest Measurement:
{38-40}{42-44-46}"/
{96.5-101.5}{106.5-112-117} cm

Size Note: We have printed the instructions for the sizes in different colors to make it easier for you to find:

- size Small in Blue
- size Medium in Pink
- size Large in Green
- size 1X in Purple
- size 2X in Red

Instructions in Black apply to all sizes.

Gauge Information

With larger size needles,
in ribbed pattern (Rows 5 & 6),
16 sts and 16 rows = 4" (10 cm)

Techniques Used

- Increasing Evenly Spaced ***(page 45)***
- Increases ***(pages 45 & 46)***
- Decreases ***(pages 46 & 47)***

Back
With Color A and larger size needles, cast on {78-82}{86-90-94} sts.

Rows 1-4: Beginning with a **purl** row, work in Stockinette Stitch.

Row 5: P2, (K2, P2) across.

Row 6 (Right side)**:** K2, (P2, K2) across.

Repeat Rows 5 and 6 for ribbed pattern until Back measures approximately {8-8}{8¼-8½-8¾}"/{20.5-20.5}{21-21.5-22} cm from bottom of rolled edge.

With Color B, work even until Back measures approximately {15¾-16}{16½-17-17½}"/{40-40.5}{42-43-44.5} cm from bottom of rolled edge.

With Color C, work even until Back measures approximately {22-22½}{23-24-24½}"/{56-57}{58.5-61-62} cm from bottom of rolled edge, ending by working Row 5.

Shoulder Shaping
Note: Maintain established pattern throughout.

Rows 1-4: Bind off {9-9}{10-10-11} sts at the beginning of the row, work across: {42-46}{46-50-50} sts.

Rows 5 and 6: Bind off {8-10}{9-11-11} sts at the beginning of the row, work across: {26-26}{28-28-28} sts.

Slip remaining sts onto st holder.

Front
Work same as Back until Front measures approximately {19-19½}{20-21-21½}"/{48.5-49.5}{51-53.5-54.5} cm from bottom of rolled edge, ending by working Row 5.

Neck Shaping
Note: Both sides of Neck are worked at the same time, using separate yarn for **each** side. Maintain established pattern throughout.

Row 1: Work across {32-34}{35-37-39} sts, slip next {14-14}{16-16-16} sts onto st holder; with second yarn, work across: {32-34}{35-37-39} sts **each** side.

Row 2: Work across to within 2 sts of Neck edge, decrease; with second yarn, decrease, work across: {31-33}{34-36-38} sts **each** side.

Row 3 (Decrease row)**:** Work across to within 2 sts of Neck edge, decrease; with second yarn, decrease, work across: {30-32}{33-35-37} sts **each** side.

Row 4: Work across; with second yarn, work across.

Rows 5-12: Repeat Rows 3 and 4, 4 times: {26-28}{29-31-33} sts **each** side.

Shoulder Shaping

Rows 1-4: Bind off {9-9}{10-10-11} sts at Armhole edge, work across; with second yarn, work across: {8-10}{9-11-11} sts **each** side.

Row 5: Bind off remaining sts on first side; with second yarn, work across.

Bind off remaining sts.

Sleeve (Make 2)

Color Sequence

Work {5½-5¾}{5¾-6-6}"/{14-14.5}{14.5-15-15} cm with Color A, {5¾-5¾}{5¾-6-6¼}"/{14.5-14.5}{14.5-15-16} cm with Color B, and complete Sleeve with Color C.

With larger size needles , cast on 30 sts.

Rows 1-4: Beginning with a **purl** row, work in Stockinette Stitch.

Row 5: Purl across increasing 6 sts evenly spaced: 36 sts.

Rows 6 and 7: (K2, P2) across.

Beginning with the next row and working new stitches in ribbed pattern, increase one stitch at **each** edge, every other row, {3-6}{10-13-16} times; then increase every fourth row, {13-12}{10-9-8} times: {68-72}{76-80-84} sts.

Work even until Sleeve measures approximately {17-17½}{17½-18-18½}"/{43-44.5}{44.5-45.5-47} cm from bottom of rolled edge.

Bind off all sts in pattern.

Finishing

Sew shoulder seams.

Neck Edging

With **right** side facing and Color C, slip {26-26}{28-28-28} sts from Back st holder onto circular needle and knit across, pick up 16 sts evenly spaced along left Front Neck edge *(Fig. 12b, page 47)*, slip {14-14}{16-16-16} sts from Front st holder onto second end of circular needle and knit across, pick up 16 sts evenly spaced along right Front Neck edge, place marker to indicate the beginning of rnd *(see Markers, page 45)*: {72-72}{76-76-76} sts.

Knit 7 rnds.

Bind off all sts **loosely** in **knit**.

Sew Sleeves to Sweater, matching center of last row on Sleeve to shoulder seam and beginning {8½-9}{9½-10-10½}"/{21.5-23}{24-25.5-26.5} cm down from seam.

Weave underarm and side in one continuous seam *(Fig. 13, page 47)*.

BACK

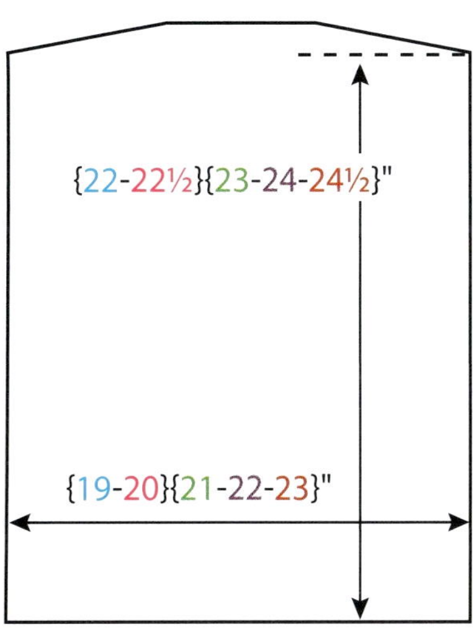

FRONT

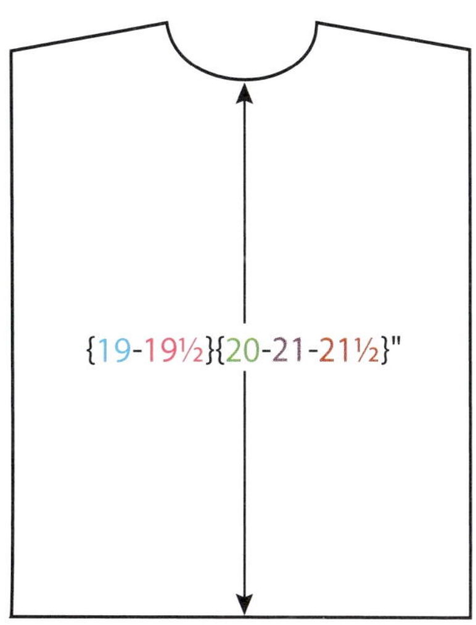

SLEEVE

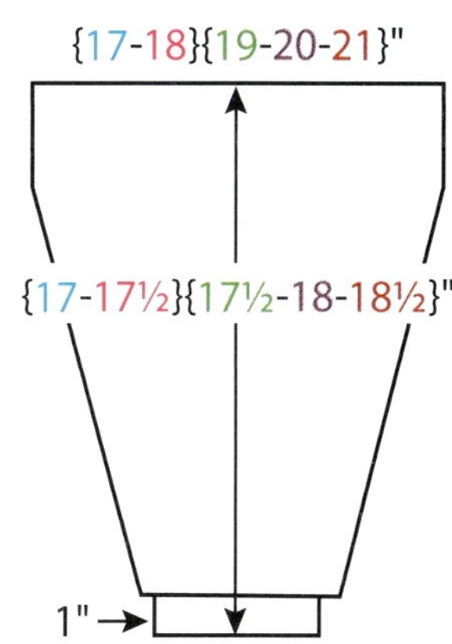

General Instructions

Knitting Needles																			
U.S.	0	1	2	3	4	5	6	7	8	9	10	10½	11	13	15	17	19	35	50
U.K.	13	12	11	10	9	8	7	6	5	4	3	2	1	00	000	---	---	---	---
Metric - mm	2	2.25	2.75	3.25	3.5	3.75	4	4.5	5	5.5	6	6.5	8	9	10	12.75	15	19	25

Abbreviations

- **CC** Contrasting Color
- **cm** centimeters
- **K** knit
- **MC** Main Color
- **mm** millimeters
- **P** purl
- **PSSO** pass slipped stitch over
- **Rnd(s)** Round(s)
- **st(s)** stitch(es)
- **tbl** through back loop(s)
- **tog** together
- **WYB** with yarn in back
- **WYF** with yam in front
- **YO** yarn over

BASIC	Projects using basic stitches. May include basic increases and decreases.
EASY	Projects may include simple stitch patterns, color work, and/or shaping.
INTERMEDIATE	Projects may include involved stitch patterns, color work, and/or shaping.
COMPLEX	Projects may include complex stitch patterns, color work, and/or shaping using a variety of techniques and stitches simultaneously.

Knit Terminology	
UNITED STATES	**INTERNATIONAL**
gauge	= tension
bind off	= cast off
yarn over (YO)	= yarn forward (yfwd) **or** yarn around needle (yrn)

Symbols & Terms

★ — work instructions following ★ as many **more** times as indicated in addition to the first time.

( ) or [ ] — work enclosed instructions **as many** times as specified by the number immediately following **or** contains explanatory remarks.

colon (:) — the number(s) given after a colon at the end of a row or round denote(s) the number of stitches you should have on that row or round.

work even — work without increasing or decreasing in the established pattern.

Yarn Weight Symbol & Names	LACE 0	SUPER FINE 1	FINE 2	LIGHT 3	MEDIUM 4	BULKY 5	SUPER BULKY 6	JUMBO 7
Type of Yarns in Category	Fingering, size 10 crochet thread	Sock, Fingering, Baby	Sport, Baby	DK, Light Worsted	Worsted, Afghan, Aran	Chunky, Craft, Rug	Super Bulky, Roving	Jumbo, Roving
Knit Gauge Ranges in Stockinette St to 4" (10 cm)	33-40 sts**	27-32 sts	23-26 sts	21-24 sts	16-20 sts	12-15 sts	7-11 sts	6 sts and fewer
Advised Needle Size Range	000 to 1	1 to 3	3 to 5	5 to 7	7 to 9	9 to11	11 to 17	17 and larger

* GUIDELINES ONLY: The chart above reflects the most commonly used gauges and needle sizes for specific yarn categories.

** Lace weight yarns are usually knitted on larger needles to create lacy openwork patterns. Accordingly, a gauge range is difficult to determine. Always follow the gauge stated in your pattern.

Gauge

Exact gauge is essential for proper fit. Before beginning your sweater, make a sample swatch in the yarn and needle specified. After completing the swatch, measure it, counting your stitches and rows carefully. If your swatch is larger or smaller than specified, make another, changing needle size to get the correct gauge. Keep trying until you find the size needles that will give you the specified gauge. Once proper gauge is obtained, measure width of garment approximately every 3" to be sure gauge remains consistent.

Sizing
When choosing what size to make, you may want to measure a favorite sweater with similar styling and knit the size that has the nearest finished measurement. Once you have chosen a size, you may adjust the body length and the sleeve length to accommodate the actual measurements while adjusting the amount of yarn purchased accordingly.

Markers
As a convenience to you, we have used markers to help distinguish the beginning of a pattern or the beginning of a round. Place markers as instructed. You may use purchased markers or tie a length of contrasting color yarn around the needle . When you reach a marker on each row or round, slip it from the left needle to the right needle; remove it when no longer needed.

Basic Stitches
Stockinette Stitch
Knit one row (right side), purl one row. The knit side is smooth and flat *(Fig. 1a)*, and the purl side is bumpy *(Fig 1b)*.

Fig. 1a

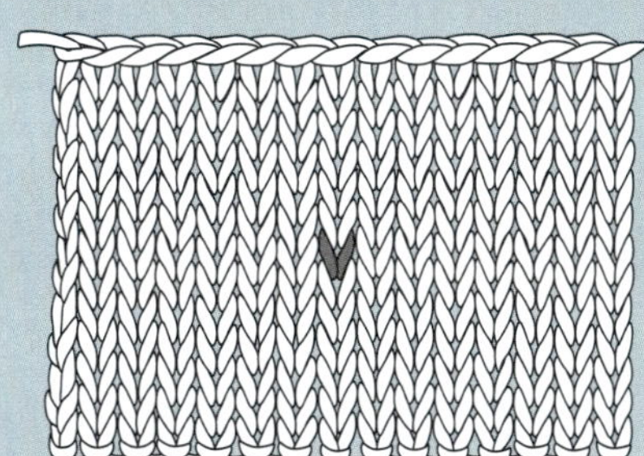

Fig. 1b

Reverse Stockinette Stitch
Reverse Stockinette Stitch is worked the same as Stockinette Stitch with the exception that the **purl** side of your fabric is considered to be the right side.

Zeros
To consolidate the length of an involved pattern, zeros are sometimes used so that all sizes can be combined. For example, P2{0-1} means size Small would P2, size Medium would do nothing, and size Large would P1.

Increases
Increasing Evenly Across A Row
Add one to the number of increases required and divide that number into the number of stitches on the needle. Subtract one from the result and the new number is the approximate number of stitches to be worked between each increase. Adjust the number as needed.

Knit Increase

Knit the next stitch but do **not** slip the old stitch off the left needle ***(Fig. 2a)***. Insert the right needle into the **back** loop of the **same** stitch and knit it ***(Fig. 2b)***, then slip the old stitch off the left needle.

Fig. 2a

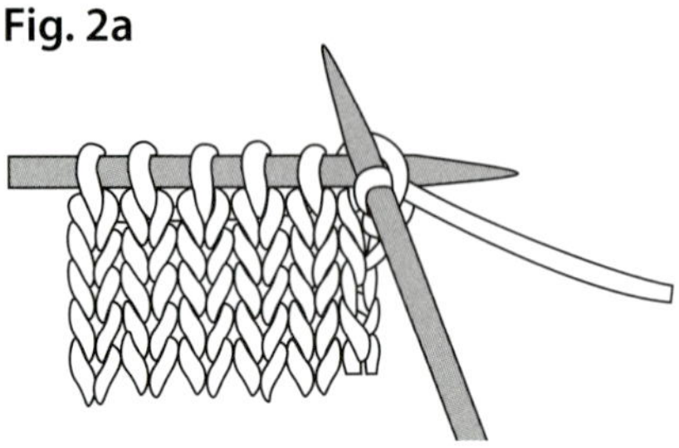

Fig. 2b

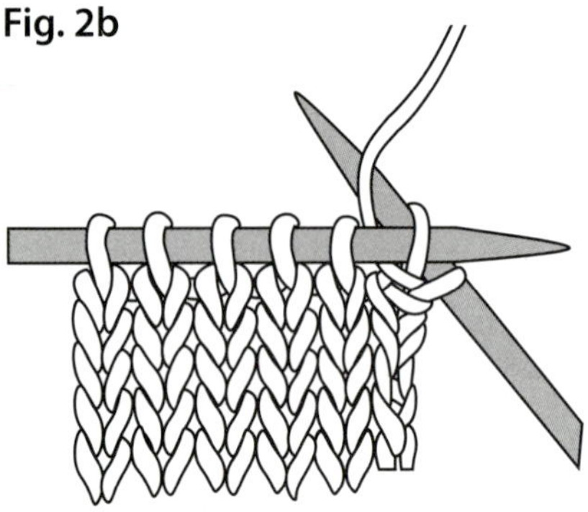

Purl Increase

Purl the next stitch but do **not** slip the old stitch off the left needle. Insert the right needle into the **back** loop of the **same** stitch from **back** to **front** ***(Fig. 3)*** and purl it. Slip the old stitch off the left needle.

Fig. 3

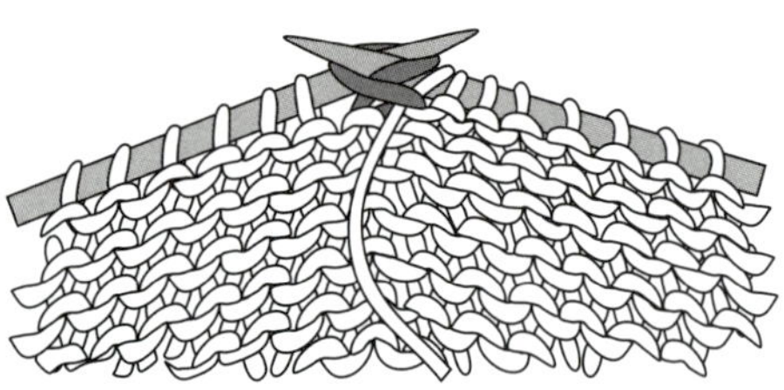

Yarn Over

Bring the yam forward **between** the needles, then back **over** the top of the right hand needle, so that it is now in position to knit the next stitch ***(Fig. 4)***.

Fig. 4

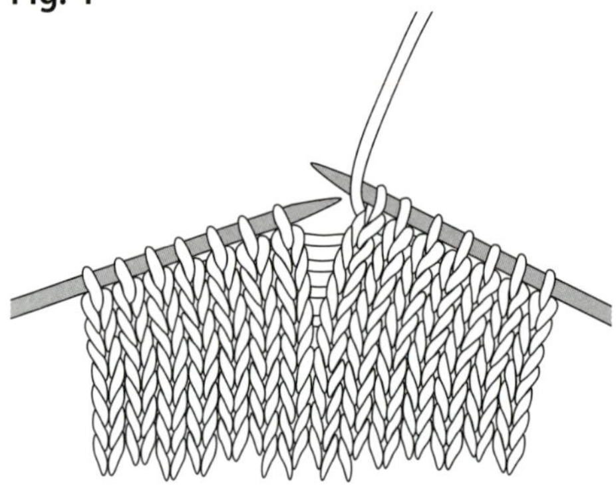

Adding New Stitches

Insert the right needle into the stitch as if to **knit**, yam over and pull loop through ***(Fig. 5a)***, insert the left needle into the loop just worked from **front** to **back** and slip the loop onto the left needle ***(Fig. 5b)***. Repeat for required number of stitches.

Fig. 5a

Fig. 5b

Decreases

Knit 2 Together

(abbreviated K2 tog)

Insert the right needle into the **front** of the first two stitches on the left needle as if to **knit** ***(fig. 6)***, Then **knit** them together as if they were one stitch.

Fig. 6

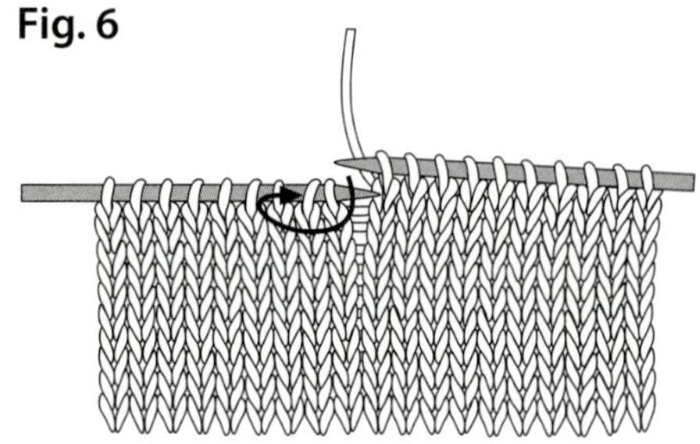

Knit 4 Together

(abbreviated K4 tog)

Insert the right needle into the **front** of the first four stitches on the left needle as if to **knit** ***(Fig. 7)***, then **knit** them together as if they were one stitch.

Fig. 7

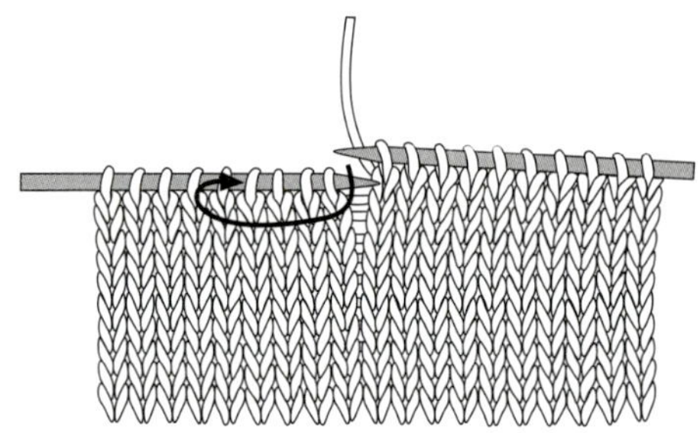

Slip 1, Knit 1, Pass Slipped Stitch Over

(abbreviated slip 1, K1, PSSO)

Slip one stitch as if to **knit** ***(Fig. 8a)***. Knit the next stitch. With the left needle, bring the slipped stitch over the knit stitch ***(Fig. 8b)*** and off the needle.

Fig. 8a

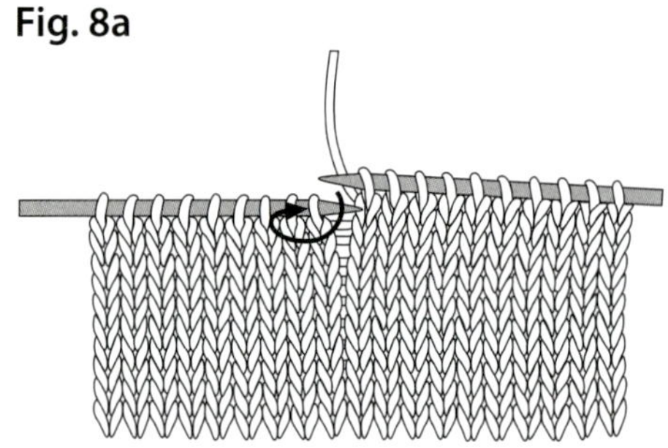

Fig. 8b

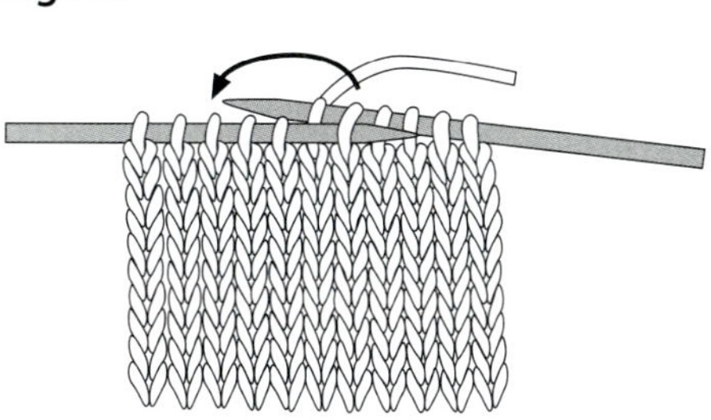

Slip 1, Knit 2 Together, Pass Slipped Stitch Over *(abbreviated slip 1, K2 tog, PSSO)*

Slip one stitch as if to knit *(Fig. 8a, page 46)*, then knit the next two stitches together *(Fig. 6, page 46)*. With the left needle, bring the slipped stitch over the stitch just made *(Fig. 9)* and off the needle.

Fig. 9

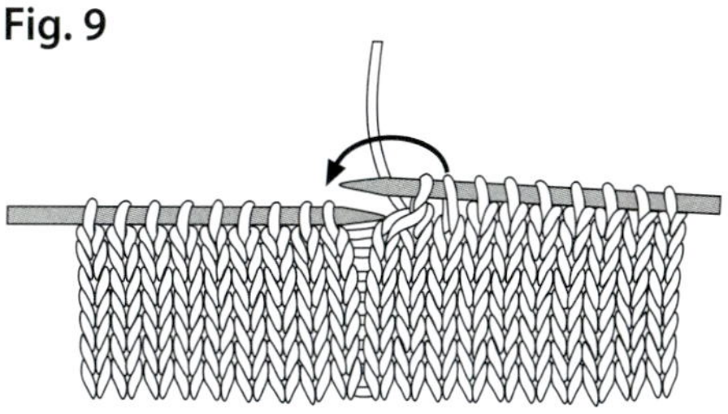

Purl 2 Together *(abbreviated P2 tog)*

Insert the right needle into the **front** of the first two stitches on the left needle as if to **purl** *(Fig. 10)*, then **purl** them together as if they were one stitch.

Fig. 10

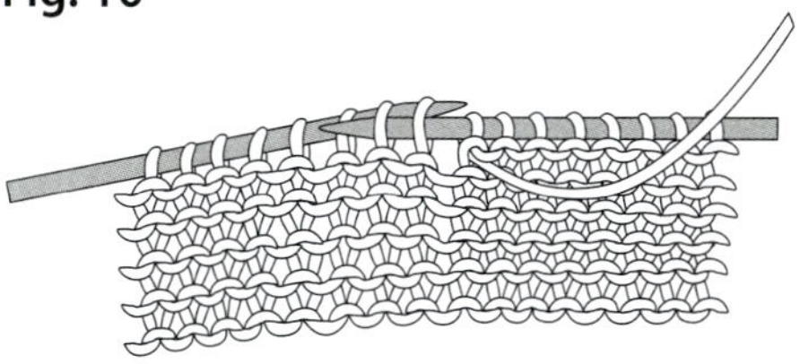

Purl 2 Together Through Back Loop *(abbreviated P2 tog tbl)*

Insert the right needle into the **back** loop of the next two stitches from **back** to **front** *(Fig. 11)*, then **purl** them together as if they were one stitch.

Fig. 11

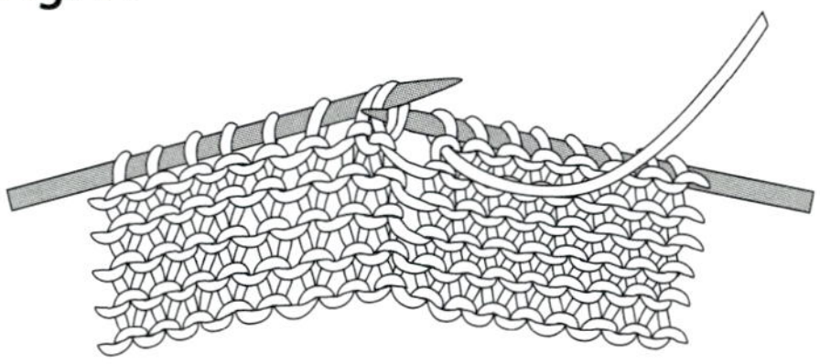

Picking Up Stitches

When instructed to pick up stitches, insert the needle from the **front** to the **back** under two strands at the edge of the worked piece *(Figs. 12a & b)*. Wrap the yarn around the needle as if to **knit**, then bring the needle with the yarn back through the stitch to the right side, resulting in a stitch on the needle.

Repeat this along the edge, picking up the required number of stitches.

A crochet hook may be helpful to pull yarn through.

Fig. 12a

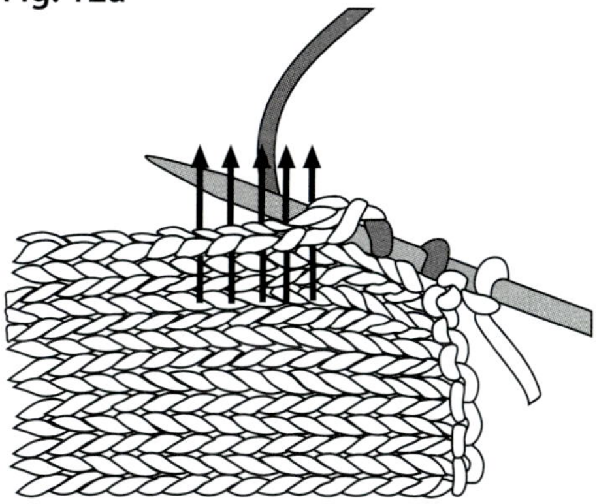

Fig. 12b

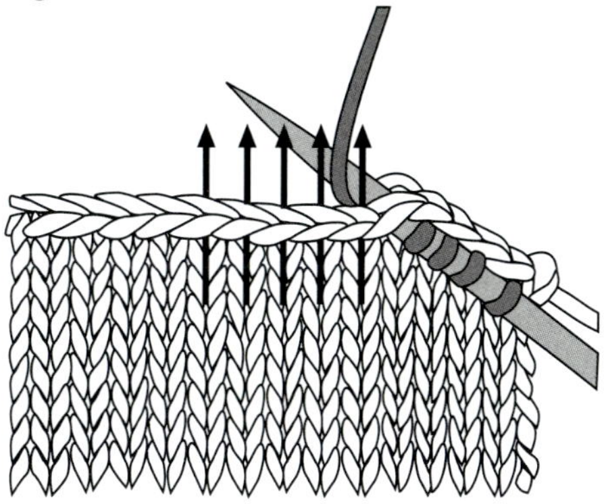

Weaving Seams

With the **right** side of both pieces facing you and edges even, sew through both sides once to secure the seam. Insert the needle under the bar **between** the first and second stitches on the row and pull the yam through *(Fig. 13)*. Insert the needle under the next bar on the second side. Repeat from side to side, being careful to match rows and drawing seam together as you work. If the edges are different lengths, it may be necessary to insert the needle under two bars at one edge.

Fig. 13

Yarn Information

The Sweaters in this book were made using Lion Brand® Homespun®, a Bulky Weight yarn. Any brand of Bulky Weight yarn may be used. It is best to refer to the yardage/meters when determining how many balls or skeins to purchase. Remember, to arrive at the finished size, it is the GAUGE/TENSION that is important, not the brand of yarn.

For your convenience, listed below are the specific colors used to create our photography models. Because yarn manufacturers make frequent changes in their product lines, you may sometimes find it necessary to use a substitute yarn or to search for the discontinued product at alternate suppliers (locally or online).

**discontinued color

Hooded Pullover
1a. #319 Adirondack**
1b. #304 Country**

Hooded Zippered Cardigan
#307 Antique**

Funnel Neck Pullover
#309 Deco

Cardigan Vest
MC - #311 Rococo
CC - #321 Williamsburg**

Cowl Neck Tunic
#300 Hepplewhite

Rugby Pullover
MC (Tan) - #311 Rococo
CC (Blue) - #302 Colonial

Scoop Neck Pullover
#302 Colonial

Lacy Pullover
#300 Hepplewhite

Ribbed Pullover - Solid Version
#309 Deco

Ribbed Pullover - Striped Version
Color A (Brown) - #326 Ranch
Color B (Variegated) -
#319 Adirondack**
Color C (Off White) - #309 Deco

Production Team: Project Manager/Technical Editor - Linda A. Daley, Graphic Artist - Kate Moul, Photo Stylist - Lori Wenger, and Photographer - Jason Masters.

Made in U.S.A.